Step-By-Step Guide to Your Retirement Security

Step-By-Step Guide to Your Retirement Security

Jack Melnick

 Times BOOKS

Copyright © 1978 by Jack Melnick

All rights reserved, including the right to reproduce this book or portions thereof in any form. For information, address: Times Books, a division of Quadrangle/The New York Times Book Company, Inc., Three Park Avenue, New York, N.Y. 10016.

Manufactured in the United States of America. Published simultaneously in Canada by Fitzhenry & Whiteside, Ltd., Toronto.

Designed by Beth Tondreau

Library of Congress Catalog Card Number: 77-87831

International Standard Book Number: 0-8129-0752-3

To my mother, Hassie, whose retirement gave me the first practical test of the principles in this book; to my children, Gail and Richard, whose college costs demanded solution; and to my wife, Diana, who will have to put up with me after we retire.

CONTENTS

1. **WHO IS THIS BOOK FOR?**   13

    At what investment stage are you?   13
    1. Speculation   13
    2. Goal-directed investment   14
        The "Rule of 72"   14
    3. Investment for assured retirement income   15
        Social Security   15
        Company retirement plans   15
        Your own retirement plans: IRA; Keogh;
            and annuities   15
        Your own resources   16
    What this book *can't* do   16
    What this book *can* do   17

2. **APPROXIMATING EXPENSES**   18

    Determining expenses today   18
    Projecting "milestone" events and future cost trends   18
    Primary expenses   18
        Housing   19
        Taxes and payroll deductions   19
        Utilities   19
        Insurance   19
        Contributions   19
        Medical   19
        Household expenses   19
        Transportation   19
        Personal needs   19
        Recreation   19
        Education   19
        Debts   19
        Miscellaneous   19
        Savings   19
    EXHIBIT I. EXPENSE APPROXIMATER (SAMPLE)   22

3. FIRST CUT AT A RETIREMENT PLAN

    Non-income-producing assets 23
        Your home 23
        Your vehicles 23
        Your vacation lot 23
        Your vacation home 23
        Your jewelry, furs, and other valuables 23
    Converting to liquid assets 24
Income-producing assets: bank accounts, stocks, and bonds 24
Income sources not from assets 24
    A. Social Security 25
        History of Social Security maximum earnings and individual contributions (Table I) 26
        Approximate Social Security annual retirement benefits (Table II) 27
        Social Security calculations (Table III) 28
        Social Security's return on investment 29
        When to start collecting 29
        Actuarial table (Table IV) 30
    B. Company retirement plans or pensions 30
        Non-contributory plans 30
        Contributory plans 30
        Joint and survivors options 31
    C. Annuities and retirement income insurance 31
        Single-premium deferred annuities 32
Completing the Retirement Plan 33
    Income-producing assets 33
    Taxability 33
    Financial assumptions used in planning 34
        Home 34
        Cost-of-living 34
        Salary after retirement 34
        Legacies 34
        Interest calculations 34
    Estimating final salary 34
    Capital gains, dividends, certificates of deposit, E bonds, and H bonds 35
    Personal resources assets 36
    Company retirement benefits 36
    Social Security benefits 36

Totaling up 36
EXHIBIT II. RETIREMENT PLAN (SAMPLE) — FIRST CUT 37

4. USING THE TAX ESTIMATER 38

Picking up income data and determining
  deductions, taxable income, and tax rate 38
Taxable federal income tax rates (Table V) 39
Calculating federal income tax 40
Calculating state income tax 40
Finishing up the Expense Approximater 40
EXHIBIT III. TAX ESTIMATER (SAMPLE) 41

5. NOW, LET'S GET SERIOUS! 42

Prioritizing needs 42
    Necessary and mandatory 42
    Desirable 42
    Nice to have 42
Trade-offs 43
A. Stashing it away for college 43
  What a college education will cost 43
  Put aside before college starts 44
  Uniform gifts to minors 44
    Tax benefits to donors 45
  The first financial plan: providing education
    for your children 48
B. Stashing it away for yourself 48
  11 saving tricks 48
    1. FICA deductions assumed for the
      full year 48
    2. Loose change 50
    3. Expense accounts 50
    4. Credit unions 50
    5. Employee stock purchase plans 50
    6. Interest on demand deposits 50
EXHIBIT IV. AVERAGE COLLEGE COST CALCULATOR 51
    7. Taking advantage of billing cycles 52
    8. E bond purchases through payroll savings 52
    9. Money market funds 53
    10. Municipal bond funds 53
    11. Withholding tax 54

C. Sources of "new" money 56
   1. Unused vacation time 56
   2. Increasing return on investment 57
   3. Building assets by tax savings 58
      The effect of federal income taxes 58
      Real interest rates on taxable income (Table VI) 59
      Taxes and real return on investments 60
   4. Your insurance policies 62
      Equivalent interest rates on non-taxable investments (Table VII) 63
      The real purpose of life insurance 64
      Insurance as a savings account? 64
      Borrowing against life insurance? 65
      Converting life insurance to term insurance and savings 66
      Comparison of 3 plans of term insurance (Table VIII) 67
      Receiving your benefits *before* you die 67
   5. Discount bonds 68
      The nature of bonds: real growth vehicles 68
      Calculating the return on discount bonds 68
      How bond prices are quoted 69
      Callable bonds 69
      Commissions on bonds 70
      Insurance for municipal bonds 70
   6. "Liquifying" your home 70
      Second mortgage trusts and second mortgages: Do they pay? 71
      Refinancing your home: a modest income opportunity 72
   7. Some new approaches to mortgage financing 73
   8. The "senior citizen" advantage 73
D. Filling out the Sources of "New" Money form 75
EXHIBIT V. SOURCES OF "NEW" MONEY (SAMPLE) 76

6. SMOOTHING OUT THE RETIREMENT PLAN 78

Effect of "new" money on short-fall 78
   1. Income grows 78
   2. Return on investment improves 78
   3. Amount of taxable income decreases 79
   4. Estate taxes are minimal 79

"Flower bonds" 80
EXHIBIT VI. RETIREMENT PLAN (SAMPLE) — SMOOTHED OUT 81

7. DEVELOPING A FINANCIAL PLAN OF ACTION 82

Too little planning — a widespread problem 82
What is a Plan of Action? 83
Checklist of planning actions (Table IX) 83–84
EXHIBIT VII. FINANCIAL PLAN OF ACTION (SAMPLE) 85

8. GETTING PROFESSIONAL HELP WHEN YOU NEED IT 87

The cost of advice 87
Kinds of help you can get (Table X) 88
Attorney 88
Investment advisor 88
Accountant 88
Banking institution 88
Insurance agent 88
Company personnel department 89
Social Security Administration 89

9. INCREASING RETIREMENT INCOME 90

Principles for retirement income 90
High-income, safe-return investments 90
For $1000 or less 90
U.S. Treasury notes 91
U.S. Series H bonds 91
U.S. Government agency securities 91
Savings certificates 91
Unit investment trusts 91
For $1000–5000 92
Municipal bond funds 92
Municipal bonds 92
U.S. Government agency securities 93
Utility stocks 93
Preferrred stocks 93
Corporate bonds 93
Thrift certificates 94
For $10,000 94
U.S. Treasury bills 94
U.S. Government agency securities 94

  For $25,000 94
   Government National Mortgage
    Association securities 94
  For $100,000 95
   Certificates of deposit 95
   Commercial paper 95
   Banker's acceptances 95
   Money market funds 95
More speculative investments 95
  Selling "covered" options 95
  "Naked" options are a no-no 96
  How options work 96
Liquidity, emergency reserves, and investment reserves 97
The row over mandatory retirement 97

APPENDIX 101

 Tables and worksheets 101
  Table A. Effective rates of compound
   interest 102
  Table B. Compounded amount on $1.00
   at various interest rates 102
  Table C. Accumulated amount on $1.00
   deposits at the beginning of each year
   at various interest rates 103–104
  Table D. Estate and gift tax rate table 104
 Highlights of the Employee Retirement
  Income Security Act of 1974 (ERISA) 105
  A. Qualification of the plan 105
  B. Eligibility of employees 106
  C. Vested retirement rights 106
  D. Funding of the plan 107
  E. Portability of benefits 108
  F. Annual benefits 108
  G. Plan termination insurance 108
  H. Reporting provisions 109
  Brief glossary of terms 109
PERSONAL RESOURCES RECORD (WORKSHEETS) 111–138
EXHIBIT I WORKSHEET. EXPENSE APPROXIMATER
EXHIBIT III WORKSHEET. TAX ESTIMATER
EXHIBIT V WORKSHEET. SOURCES OF "NEW" MONEY

1. Who is this book for?

Have you ever heard the saying "It's never too late?" *Don't believe it*—especially if you have ever felt concern for the quality of your life after retirement, or for the financial well being of your loved ones. The truth is, it is *never to early* to plan for retirement.

People who are not 5-15 years away from mandatory retirement or voluntary early retirement may not become excited about the contents of this book. They should, for two very good reasons:

1. Your two biggest assets for successful retirement— *time and compound interest*— will work for you longer if you start now.
2. The earlier you start, the greater your *flexibility* of investment choice will be.

People generally go through three investment stages. This book is really for people who have been fed up by the first investment stage and are entering or have entered stage two. If you haven't done any planning and are in, or about to enter, stage three, it may be already too late for you to get much help from this book. However, Chapter 9 on Increasing Retirement Income will still make worthwhile reading.

The first stage is *speculative and non-goal directed* (or the "crap shooting" phase), where people leap at hot stock tips, buy lottery tickets, or hope to "break the bank" at Monte Carlo. They have no clear objective; they take chances and hope they'll hit it lucky. They have no clear idea what they'll do with the money, even if they make it. The fun is in trying. There is no age range for people in this investment stage, but they generally range from the twenties through the mid-forties.

As a rule, most people "just can't pick 'em." Don't feel bad; the experts have trouble, too. Consider the stock market slumps of recent years, the constant switching between securities that mutual funds, insurance companies, and pension funds indulge in, and the often unpredictable fluctuations in the stock "averages" such as Dow-Jones and Industrials. Real estate investment trusts were the rage for a few years—until they collapsed. Then came money market funds, followed by this gimmick, then that fad. What's an investor to do? Even the safest of mutual funds, the best investment management, the most

At what investment stage are you?

1. SPECULATION

highly respected analysts, often "call them wrong." How can John Q. Investor hope to do better than these experts whose very recommendations or reactions may cause aberrations in stock, gold, or other financial markets? Fortunately for most people, the losses possible in the speculative stage are contained and restricted by the limited amounts of capital available to younger investors.

2. GOAL-DIRECTED INVESTMENT

Most people mature into the second investment stage when faced with some realities. "How can I afford to send my kids to college?" "Can I afford to retire? And when?" "How come all my investments go sour?" This second investment stage begins with the realization that you need *investment goals that will assure capital growth.* At the same time, you begin to allow for *investment flexibility* to offset the ravages of inflation. The money *must* be there when you need it. You *must* be assured that capital will increase to the level you need. You therefore begin to consider the need for a balanced investment portfolio, even if it's just a modest portfolio. This book is for these folks.

The "Rule of 72"

The prime rule to remember in this stage is the "rule of 72." In simple form, you can calculate the number of years it takes a fixed sum to double in value by dividing the number "72" by the growth rate you are receiving for your money. For example, if your growth rate is 8%, calculate "72 divided by 8"; your money will double in 9 years. At 6% growth, your money will double in 12 years. It follows that if you double your money in 12 years, you will quadruple it in 24 years, and octuple it in 36 years. The successful goal-directed capital acquirer must trade off the many investment opportunities that will come his way against this formula. (See the Appendix for more on this subject.)

Given a fixed period of time, what is the best method of guaranteeing maximum capital growth? What is the likelihood that a given speculative investment can match the capital growth possible from insured savings, just using the "rule of 72"? If you have, say, 24 years to retirement, and you can get an assured 6% return on investment, you can quadruple your capital by retirement. Now, what is the likelihood that an alternative investment—such as a stock, a real estate investment, a gold bar, or a rare coin or stamp, will be worth over four times what was paid for it in 24 years? To the goal-directed investor, this becomes a serious question.

3. INVESTMENT FOR ASSURED RETIREMENT INCOME

The goals of the second investment stage eventually lead into one ultimate goal at the third stage—*assured income from investment.* Essentially, when you retire, you'll be forced to live on income from a limited number of sources:

- Social Security
- Company retirement plans
- Your own retirement plan
- Your own resources and savings
- Post-retirement earnings, rentals, etc.

None of these sources is likely to provide a worry-free, independent retirement income by itself.

Social Security

Although Social Security payments are often increased by Congress, the Social Security program is not intended to satisfy all retirement needs. First of all, it can't begin yielding benefits earlier than age 62; secondly, maximum benefits are limited by covered earned income, not total income. In 1977, for example, the maximum was based on $16,500 of earned income, regardless of the total personal income actually earned, dividends or interest received, etc. (See Chapter 3 for more Social Security information.)

Company retirement plans

Company retirement plans, where they can be relied upon, provide retirement income keyed to either length of service or personal earnings or both. Typically, the retirement benefits provided will be a percentage of pre-retirement earnings ranging from 25–60% or more of your last annual salary. Such plans often contain provisions for "joint and survivor" income, which provides for the surviving spouse if the wage earner dies first after retirement begins.

Your own retirement plans: IRA; Keogh; and annuities

Individuals can set up their own retirement plan if they work for a company that does not provide a retirement program or if they are self-employed. For the employee without a company plan, the Individual Retirement Account (IRA) permits up to $1500 or 15% of earned income per year (whichever is smaller) to be invested. There are two kinds of savings available from IRA. First, the actual amount deposited is deducted from gross pay; in other words, it is "sheltered" for income tax purposes. Second, the interest earned from your retirement account is not taxed until it is withdrawn (but only if it is not withdrawn before age 59½). Very attractive interest rates are obtainable for IRA accounts because of the long-term nature of the investment. The only drawbacks to IRA retirement accounts are the high penalties invoked for early withdrawal and the fact that you will not be allowed to borrow against

15

your account, that is, to use the account as collateral. You can if you wish, continue to maintain a tax shelter with your IRA plan until age 70½.

For the self-employed, the Keogh Plan (HR10) allows a deduction of up to $7500 or 15% of earnings (whichever is smaller) with the same tax exclusions as under IRA. Sheltered current earnings and deferred taxes on future earnings from that investment are common to both Keogh and IRA. During a working lifetime of 30 years, assuming maximum investment and a 7¾% interest rate, an IRA account can grow to over $183,510 and a Keogh Account to over $917,550! And all this in insured, no-risk savings.

Unfortunately, relatively few people qualify for full participation in either of these plans. And if they do qualify, few can earn the $10,000 or $50,000 per year, every year, to assure maximum participation in IRA or Keogh. Improvements are made in these plans occasionally, as the change of 1976 allowing joint husband/wife combination to shelter even more—up to $1750—even if one partner was not working at all.

Other types of non-company retirement plans include annuities, which generally offer a greater, safer return, but sometimes mean your heirs will forego the remaining principal. If you have no heirs, or if they don't need to inherit your estate, an annuity may be useful to increase your return from a specific sum of money and will provide an income that you will not outlive. Incidentally, there is nothing shameful about spending some of your capital to augment your own income in retirement. Where is it written that retired persons have to deny themselves just to assure an estate for their children?

Your own resources

The last item, your own resources—and savings, post-retirement earnings, rentals and so forth—will occupy most of the pages of this book.

What this book can't do

Now, there are some things this book does not cover. These are the *personal* questions that you'll have to resolve in your own mind and with your own family. Some of these include:
- Given the opportunity, should you retire early?
- What will you do with yourself after retirement?
- Should you get a job after retirement?
- Where can you get a job after retirement?
- Can you become a consultant?
- To move, or not to move?
- Where might you move?
- Should you sell your house?
- What is your spouse going to do?

Similarly, this book cannot go into great lengths about *estate planning*. There are several fine texts on this subject already available, and the Tax Reform Act of 1976 changed the ground rules so dramatically that many people will not have estates large enough to pay significant estate taxes. Therefore, this book will not go into estate planning other than to the extent that retirement planning is an adjunct to estate planning. (See Table D in the Appendix for estate and gift tax rates.)

The following chapters will look in depth at the *financial* aspects of retirement. When you have finished reading them, you'll be capable of intelligently evaluating and answering such questions as:

- Can you afford to retire?
- Can you retire early?
- After your children graduate from college, what's left for you?
- How much will you need to send your children to college?
- How should you combine the sources of retirement income?
- How can you create "new" money for retirement?
- What are conservative, secure investment programs that will provide adequate income while safeguarding your capital?

What this book *can* **do**

Retirement should be the goal toward which a person works; the fulfillment of a lifetime of work. Yet, many people fear retirement as the "end of their life," or the "beginning of the end." It certainly need not be so. With *careful planning, time,* and *goal-directed capital growth,* retirement can be a pleasant, time-of-your-life situation made possible by your life-time labor and thrift.

17

2. Approximating expenses

Determining expenses today

The basic question—"Can I afford to retire?"—can't be answered until you know what it's going to cost you to live when you retire. Now, no one can calculate the costs with certainty, so the best you can do is make an educated guess.

Your educated guess begins by determining your expenses according to your present standard of living. This is not a budgeting exercise, but a real look at where the money goes today.

Projecting "milestone" events and future cost trends

The following analysis involves tracking down, at least approximately, every expenditure out of today's income. You must then project these expenses over time, starting with the first full year after your expected date of retirement, and optionally including "milestone" event years, such as "mortgage paid off," "Social Security starts," and so on. Using all the information at your disposal, you'll have the opportunity to project what you believe to be future trends for inflation rate, consumer prices, cost of living, and other financial indexes of the times. Since the general trend in costs will probably be "up," you will find that your practical estimates will approximate reality fairly well. Of course, not everything goes "up." In fact, quite a few costs will go down after retirement. For example, the Social Security contribution, which was nearly $1000 in 1977, will terminate; federal, state, and local income taxes will probably go down; voluntary deductions from pay, such as savings bonds or stock purchases, will cease.

Primary expenses

To aid you in determining your expenses, a form for your use, called the Expense Approximater, is included in the Appendix to this book, and a sample is filled out as Exhibit I at the end of this chapter. (Note: By filling in the "Personal Resources Record" in the Appendix first, you will find it easier to complete the Expense Approximater.)

Let's look at the major expense categories in order to avoid forgetting any of your estimate. Assume, for simplicity, that state or local sales taxes are included in the expenses for each category.

Primary Category	Examples of Cost Items	Trend by Retirement
Housing	Mortgage (principal & interest)	Level
	Rent or condominium fee	Up
Taxes & payroll deductions	Real estate taxes	Up
	Federal income tax	Down
	State income tax	Down
	FICA (Social Security)	None
	Stock purchase	None
	Bond purchase	None
Utilities	Telephone	Up
	Electricity	Up
	Gas	Up
	Trash, Water & Sewer	Up
Insurance	Vehicles (including campers & trailers)	Down (children gone)
	House & personal property	Up
	Life, accident & travel	Level or down
Contributions	Church, charity & gifts	Down (except gifts to your children)
Medical	Net after insurance deducted	Level
	Medicare payments	Up
	Health insurance	Up
	Dental	Up
	Drugs (after insurance deductions & medicare)	Up
Household expenses	Food, household supplies, etc.	Down
	Family clothing	Down
	House & grounds maintenance	Up
Transportation	Vehicles (gas, service, parts & depreciation fund to save for new car)	Up
	Commuting (if not with car)	None
Personal needs	Cleaning, laundry, etc.	Level
	Lunch at work	None
Recreation	Entertainment, eating out, etc.	Level
	Vacations, & club dues	Up
Education	Tuition, room, board, fees	None
Debts	Long-term payments	Level
	Short-term payments	Down or none
Miscellaneous	Pets	Level
	One-time purchases (appliances, furniture)	Down
	Other (allowances, subscriptions, etc.)	Level
Savings	From salary, interest, & dividends (might be negative)	Up

A few of these items are worthy of further comment. Both federal and state income tax will have to be estimated. Chapter 4 will discuss a sample of the Tax Estimater form that appears in the Appendix for your use.

There is no hope for reprieve from the utilities. Face it, costs are going up; electricity, oil, coal, and gas are leading the way, with sewer and water costs close behind. Doubling or tripling what you are paying today may not be an unreasonable estimate.

The medical, dental, and drug expenses that you estimate should be net costs after payment or reimbursement to you by medical or health insurance. The initial cost of health insurance, however, excluding payments made by your employer or other reductions that have decreased your own financial outlays should be included here. Remember, when Medicare starts, a new health plan will be needed, and total costs may go down. (Tax Tip: Current federal tax laws allow deduction of one half of medical insurance payments, even if you don't qualify under the 1% drug and 3% medical deductible. Also, one half of medical insurance premiums which are part of your automobile or homeowner's policies can be included in the deduction.)

Contributions are so personal in nature, yet so controllable, that no real recommendation can be made other than to suggest that, after retirement, charity begins at home. (Tax Tip: Current federal tax laws allow deduction of charitable contributions other than cash. This includes gifts of clothing, toys, furniture, and appliances. Check your tax booklet for procedures to claim these deductions; don't just ignore them. Remember, giving away those items at Fair market value results in tax savings to you, calculated by multiplying your federal tax rate by the value of the contribution. Also, you can deduct 7 cents per mile that you travel for a charity or volunteer job.)

In the area of transportation, energy shortages will again influence costs of auto fuel and commuting by other means. In addition, the inexorable price rise for new cars, service, and parts will offset the advantage of reducing the number of cars you own after the children have gone. You might consider setting up a depreciation or "sinking" fund so that you can afford to replace a car regularly, say, every five years. The interest gained from your fund will help pay for that new car—a more pleasant prospect than borrowing money to buy it. (Don't forget to include license and vehicle registration renewal fees in your estimates.)

Recreation, depending on your tastes, can become a major consideration since you will finally have the leisure to indulge in it. The problem is, will you have the money? Since this is a discretionary item, think about it carefully before putting down a figure. Don't hesitate to modify that figure if it's out of line, particularly if it's lower than you feel comfortable with. Having fun in retirement is what you worked all your life for, remember?

Insurance is an item we'll have more to say about in Chapter 5, under the heading, Sources of "New" Money.

Although education costs are marked "none" in our sample, assuming your children have finished their education, more and more retired people are returning to the classroom—to complete that degree they never had time for, or to take that class on ceramics or literature. Don't be afraid to plug in some money for tuition at a local community college or university, if continued education is your interest.

Finally let's consider savings. Why is savings an item of expense? Because it is a debt owed to yourself and your family. It must be paid as regularly as the gas bill, the grocery bill, and the clothing store. You must set a savings objective for yourself and keep at it. It's all too easy to dismiss the need for savings "just this month." Saving is a discipline that should be learned at an early age. Even so, some people have to trick themselves to save. An easy trick is to pretend that the FICA deduction lasts all year instead of ending after you earn $17,700 (in 1978). Just assume your spendable income *doesn't* include the money you will receive after the FICA deduction ends. Instead, deposit that money in a safe investment. (Did you know that if you save $20 per week for 28 years at 7¾% interest, you'll amass over $100,000? At 6¾% it will take 30 years. Both of these time periods are well within the working lifetime of most wage earners or self-employed people. (See the Appendix, Table C, for more detail.) Although we'll talk about sources of "new" money in Chapter 5, nothing beats regular, disciplined savings. You owe it to yourself.

A typical example of the Expense Approximater follows (Exhibit I). When you complete your own form (supplied at the back of the book), leave the federal and state income taxes blank for years beyond the current one and fill them in only after calculating your income in Chapter 3 and mastering the use of the Tax Estimater in Chapter 4.

EXHIBIT I. **EXPENSE APPROXIMATER (Sample).**

Primary	Examples		Now	1st full ret. yr.	Major change years	
		Year:	1976	1985	1994*	1998**
		Age:	47	56	65	69
Housing	Mortgage, rent		2400	2400	0	0
Taxes & Payroll Deductions	Real Estate		1200	1900	2200	2500
	Federal Income		7980	3447	2234	2067
	State Income		2415	1105	742	682
	FICA		900	0	0	0
	Stock purchase		3650	0	0	0
	Bond purchase		72	0	0	0
Utilities	Telephone		360	390	400	450
	Electricity		600	650	700	750
	Gas		470	500	550	600
	Trash, water, sewer		200	250	250	300
Insurance	Vehicles		550	500	400	450
	House & Personal Property		190	200	230	260
	Life, accident & travel		440	440	310	0
Contributions	Church, charity & gifts		700	300	300	200
Medical	Net after insurance		300	500	1000	1000
	Health insurance		(company paid)			
Household	Family clothing		3000	1500	1000	1000
	Food, supplies, etc.		4680	3500	3000	3000
	House & grounds		500	800	1000	1000
Transportaion	Gas, service & depreciation		2040	2200	2200	2200
	Commuting (if not with car)		0	0	0	0
Personal needs	Cleaning, laundry, etc.		200	150	150	150
	Lunch at work		375	0	0	0
Recreation	Entertainment		1000	750	500	500
	Vacations, club dues, etc.		1100	1700	2100	2100
Education	Tuition, room, board, fees		300	0	0	0
Debts	Long & Short Term Paymts		0	0	0	0
Miscellaneous	Pets, one-time purchases, other		500	500	500	500
Savings	From salary, interest, dividends		7098	0	0	0
	Total expenses		43220	23682	19766	19709
	Annual income		43220	23494	29755	32049
	Long- or short-fall		0	−188	+9989	+12340

Federal Income / State Income: From Tax Estimater (Exhibit III)

Totals: Post after taxes are added & after income is caluclated. See Chapter 4

* Mortgage paid: extra exemption; life insurance paid.
** Spouse 65: extra exemption.

3. First cut at a retirement plan

Now that we have a handle on approximating expenses, we can next look at your income producing assets, which will not only generate continuing income for you but will also create an asset base for your estate. Then you'll be ready for a first draft of your actual retirement plan.

Non-income-producing assets

Not all assets produce income. Some, in fact, may be income "stealers." Consider the following examples.

- *Your home*—probably your biggest non-income-producing asset. It "steals" income for maintenance, property taxes, insurance, etc. However, treated as an investment, it often will rise in value.
- *Your vehicles*—non-income-producing assets that will generally decline rapidly in value (unless you've invested in a classic or antique car!) and require lots of current income to maintain, license, insure, and fuel them.
- *Your vacation lot*—that "investment" encouraged by your local land speculator, who convinced you to buy a raw lot which may or may not increase in value. Until your vacation house is built on it, it remains an income "stealer" for taxes, upkeep and mortgage payments. (Reputable realtors suggest that if you will not be building within two or three years, don't buy the lot!)
- *Your vacation home*—an income-producing-asset only if the net rental return you get for the house is greater than your annual costs to run it. However, if the truth be known, most vacation homes are non-income-producing, although they may be used as tax vehicles to reduce income taxes somewhat by deducting real estate taxes, interest, depreciation, etc.
- *Your jewelry, furs, and other valuables*—including furniture, coins, gold bars, silver, stamps, etc. These are assets which

may increase in value, but which rarely produce current income. Because of the risk involved in owning them, these valuables may actually detract from current income for insurance, maintenance, and security.

CONVERTING TO LIQUID ASSETS

There is nothing wrong with collecting non-income-producing assets. What *is* wrong is expecting these assets to be the source of income you'll need for retirement. Providing current income after retirement generally implies the need to liquidate the non-income-producing asset, that is, to sell it so it can be converted to an income-producing asset. Similarly, if you plan to use these assets as funding sources for your children's education, you may be headed for a shock. Suppose, for example, you bought gold at $200 an ounce in 1975. What is that "investment" worth today? You'll be in for a shock. Prices have ranged from $150 to $175 an ounce in 1976 and 1977. That's some investment!

Another problem is that some of these non-income-producing assets are not very negotiable. Not only do you have no guarantee they will increase in value, but even if they do increase in value, you still have no guarantee they will have increased to the levels you'll need by the time you must liquidate them. Further, some of these assets, such as antique jewelry, may never be liquidated because of real or sentimental value. What is needed is a balance of priorities between your natural craving for *things* versus your need for *income*—in effect, your life*style* versus your life *supports*.

Income-producing assets: bank accounts, stocks, and bonds

So we have to look to income-producing assets, such as bank accounts, stocks, bonds, and true investment property to produce the income you'll ultimately need. In the years before retirement, the return on these assets can be used in either of two ways: first as an augment of current income; second as an asset builder by means of compounded interest. For purposes of retirement planning, you'll want to use the latter technique—compounding the return with favorable interest arrangements.

Income sources not from assets

The Retirement Plan is little more than a spread sheet, annualized for purposes of recording and comparing income-producing assets and the income produced by those assets. Even as there are assets which do not provide income, so there are also sources of retirement income which do not come from your assets. There are three basic sources of such income: (A) Social Security; (B) company retirement plans; and (C) annuities. Each source deserves some elaboration here.

Although you have regularly contributed to the Social Security fund, the dollars contributed are not available to you in a lump sum, but only as monthly income after a certain age, based on your average Social Security earnings over the years.

A. SOCIAL SECURITY

To help you estimate Social Security benefits, review the history of Social Security earnings and contributions in Table I. Average earnings are calculated by dividing the total Social Security earnings by the number of years covered. To determine the number of years of coverage, count from 1956, if you were born before 1930, or count from the year that you became 27 years of age if you were born after 1929. To determine your average earnings, list all social security earnings starting with 1951. Cross off the lowest earnings years until earnings years equal number of "years for count." (Table III). Add up the earnings for the years left and divide by the number of years you used. The result is the average yearly earnings. Look on the table listing approximate retirement benefits (Table II) to estimate annual benefit. (The effect of the formula is to eliminate the lowest 5 earnings years. These may very well be years of no earnings which would result with early retirement at age 55, since 7 years of no earnings would result before you could receive Social Security benefits at age 62. In an early retirement situation, it would pay to drop 5 of the 7 years of no Social Security earnings.) An example of the Social Security calculation for a person born in 1921 shows:

Number of years needed — 27 (Table III)
Total Social Security Earnings for Retirement at ages: (Add up from Table I)

	Age 65	Age 62	Age 55 (collect at age 62)
	$423,300 (1960-86)	$327,200 (1957-83)	$174,600 (1950-76)
Divide by:	÷ 27	÷ 27	÷ 27
Average Social Security earnings	$ 15,863	$ 12,118	$ 6,466
Approximate benefit (from Table II)	$ 8,553	$ 5,557	$ 3,451

25

TABLE I. HISTORY OF SOCIAL SECURITY MAXIMUM EARNINGS AND INDIVIDUAL CONTRIBUTIONS (as of Dec. 1977).

Years	Maximum S.S. Earnings	No. of Years	Individual % Rate	Annual Amount of Contribution	Total S.S. Earnings	Total S.S. Contribution
1937-1949	$ 3000	13	1.0%	$ 30.00	$ 39000	$ 390.00
1950	3000	1	1.5	45.00	3000	45.00
1951-1953	3600	3	1.5	54.00	10800	162.00
1954	3600	1	2.0	72.00	3600	72.00
1955-1956	4200	2	2.0	84.00	8400	168.00
1957-1958	4200	2	2.25	94.50	8400	189.00
1959	4800	1	2.5	120.00	4800	120.00
1960-1961	4800	2	3.0	144.00	9600	288.00
1962	4800	1	3.125	150.00	4800	150.00
1963-1965	4800	3	3.625	174.00	14400	522.00
1966	6600	1	4.2	277.00	6600	277.20
1967	6600	1	4.4	290.40	6600	290.40
1968	7800	1	4.4	343.20	7800	343.20
1969-1970	7800	2	4.8	374.40	15600	748.80
1971	7800	1	5.2	405.60	7800	405.60
1972	9000	1	5.2	468.00	9000	468.00
1973	10800	1	5.85	631.80	10800	631.80
1974	13200	1	5.85	772.20	13200	772.20
1975	14100	1	5.85	824.85	14100	824.85
1976	15300	1	5.85	895.05	15300	895.05
1977	16500	1	5.85	965.25	16500	965.25
1978	17700	1	6.05	1070.85	17700	1070.85
1979	22900	1	6.13	1403.77	22900	1403.77
1980	25900	1	6.13	1587.67	25900	1587.67
1981	29700	1	6.65	1975.05	29700	1975.05
1982	31800	1	6.7	2130.60	31800	2130.60
1983	33900	1	6.7	2271.30	33900	2271.30
1984	36000	1	6.7	2412.00	36000	2412.00
1985	38100	1	7.05	2686.05	38100	2686.05
1986	40200	1	7.15	2874.30	40200	2874.30
1987-1999	42600	13	7.15	3045.90	553800	39596.70

TABLE II. **APPROXIMATE SOCIAL SECURITY ANNUAL RETIREMENT BENEFITS (as of September 1977).**

Average S.S. Yearly Earnings	No. 1 Wage Earner Age 62	Age 65	Spouse Age 62	Age 65
$ 3000	$2143	$2678	$1004	$1339
3400	2298	2871	1077	1436
4000	2521	3151	1182	1575
4400	2701	3375	1267	1688
4800	2859	3573	1340	1786
$ 5000	$2923	$3654	$1371	$1827
5200	3006	3757	1410	1879
5400	3070	3837	1440	1918
5600	3153	3942	1479	1971
5800	3240	4048	1519	2024
$ 6000	$3303	$4129	$1549	$2065
6200	3387	4233	1587	2116
6400	3451	4314	1618	2157
6600	3534	4417	1657	2209
6800	3609	4512	1692	2256
$ 7000	$3702	$4627	$1735	$2313
7400	3870	4837	1814	2419
7600	3962	4952	1857	2476
8000	4107	5133	1926	2566
8400*	4252	5313	1993	2656
$ 8800*	$4397	$5493	$2061	$2746
9200*	4542	5673	2129	2836
9600*	4687	5853	2197	2926
10000*	4832	6033	2265	3016
10400*	4977	6213	2333	3106
$10800*	$5122	$6393	$2401	$3196
11200*	5267	6573	2469	3286
11600*	5412	6753	2537	3376
12000*	5557	6933	2605	3466
12400*	5702	7113	2668	3556
$12800*	$5847	$7293	$2736	$3646
13200*	5992	7473	2804	3736
13600*	6137	7653	2872	3826
14000*	6282	7833	2909	3916
14400*	6427	8013	3007	4006
$14800*	$6572	$8193	$3075	$4096
15200*	6717	8373	3143	4186
15600*	6862	8553	3211	4276
16000*	7007	8633	3279	4316
16400*	7152	8813	3347	4406

* Estimate

TABLE III. SOCIAL SECURITY CALCULATIONS (as of December 1977).

Year Born	Year 62	Years for Count	Average yearly earnings If Maximum Coverage	Maximum Social Security Contribution	Maximum Total Social Security Earnings
1912	1974	19	$ 6031	$ 6043.20	$ 112800
1913	1975	19	6505	6868.05	123600
1914	1976	20	6885	7763.10	137700
1915	1977	21	7285	8728.35	153000
1916	1978	22	7704	9799.20	169500
1917	1979	23*	$ 8139	$11202.97	$ 187200
1918	1980	24*	8754	12790.64	210100
1919	1981	25*	9440	14765.69	236000
1920	1982	26*	10219	16896.29	265700
1921	1983	27*	11018	19167.59	297500
1922	1984	28*	$11835	$21579.59	$ 331400
1923	1985	29*	12669	24265.64	367400
1924	1986	30*	13516	27139.94	405500
1925	1987	31*	14377	30185.84	445700
1926	1988	32*	15259	33231.74	488300
1927	1989	33*	$16088	$36277.64	$ 530900
1928	1990	34*	16867	39323.54	573500
1929	1991	35*	17602	42369.44	616100
1930	1992	35*	18820	45415.34	658700
1931	1993	35*	20037	48461.24	701300
1932	1994	35*	$21254	$51507.14	$ 743900
1933	1995	35*	22471	54553.04	786500
1934	1996	35*	23688	57598.94	829100
1935	1997	35*	24905	60644.84	871700
1936	1998	35*	26123	63690.74	914300
1937	1999	35*	$27340	$66736.64	$ 956900
1938	2000	35*	28557	69782.54	999500
1939	2001	35*	29774	72828.44	$1042100

*Estimate

Actually, considered as a return on investment, an annual Social Security benefit of $4837 at age 65 today would be equivalent to the return on $80,616.66 of investments at 6% interest, tax-free. If you retired in 1977, the maximum you could have paid into Social Security during your working years was $8728. Assuming you could have invested those payments yourself to compound at 6% interest, that investment would have grown to about $44,881. Receiving Social Security benefits equivalent to the return on $80,616 instead of interest from $44,881 is a pretty good deal. If you (1) look at Social Security as a form of *annuity* (since you may lose your capital investment if you die), and (2) consider the interest rate fluctuations over the last 40 years (2% *used* to be pretty good) as an inhibitor to your building that nest egg, and (3) reflect that income taxes would further erode your ability to build a retirement fund, and (4) consider that Social Security provided a disciplined way to save in spite of yourself, *then* the Social Security program is put in its proper perspective. It assures some income to people who otherwise would have been unable to generate retirement income on their own. The break point is currently for people born after 1926. Conceivably, a private investment plan could provide a greater return than Social Security at this point. However, taking into account the built-in cost-of-living adjustments of Social Security, it may still represent a good investment. (See Table III.)

Social Security's return on investment

A question invariably arises when you estimate your Social Security benefits. Should you start collecting at age 62, or wait until age 65 to get a larger benefit? Again, simple arithmetic comes to the rescue. Let's look at our previous example. If you started the benefit at age 62, you'd be paid about $3870 instead of $4837 per year—a difference of $967. Since for three years you would be receiving $3870, or $11,610 total, it would take $11,610 ÷ 967 or 12 years for you to reach the difference in benefits starting at age 65. The actuarial estimates are represented by Table IV.

When to start collecting

If you're a man, the odds are that you'll live 2.8 years longer than the BREAK-EVEN point, since you can be expected to live 14.8 years more. If you're a woman, you may be 4.8 years better off to wait. However, a general principle is, "take what you can get as early as you can get it." Remember, for every average, half do better and half do worse. Why deprive yourself of three years of more comfortable living for the possibility of a few more dollars three years later, when you don't know which side of the average you'll be on?

To protect your Social Security investment the Social Security Administration recommends that each covered individual request a "Statement of Wages" at least once every 3 years, without charge, from: Social Security Administration, P. O. Box 57, Baltimore, Maryland 21203.

TABLE IV. **ACTUARIAL TABLE.**

If you are now:		*You can expect to live this much longer:*
Age Male	Age Female	
59	62	16.8 years
60	63	16.1 years
61	64	15.4 years
62	65	14.8 years
63	66	14.1 years
64	67	13.5 years
65	68	12.9 years

B. COMPANY RETIREMENT PLANS OR PENSIONS

There are two main types of company retirement plans—contributory and non-contributory.

Non-contributory plans

Non-contributory plans are often set up by large corporations and are paid to eligible retiring company personnel. The retirement fund is generally separate from other corporate funds and is managed and invested to increase the assets in the fund. Typically, unless there is a vesting procedure, if the employee leaves the company prior to retirement, he gets nothing from the retirement fund. Many companies have provisions for vesting their employees, usually at 10–15 years. A vested employee, even if he leaves the company's employ, is assured of some income at age 65 or before. New laws on pension transferability have been drafted and should be frequently reviewed. (See the Appendix for information about the Employee Retirement Income Security Act—ERISA.)

Contributory plans

The contributory plans are of several sub-types. Some permit withdrawal of the amount contributed in a lump sum payment. Some will pay out on a monthly benefit basis. In most cases, however, the company retirement plan is not a recoverable asset, nor is it an asset that can be passed on to heirs through an estate.

Joint and survivors options

The closest a plan will come to aiding your beneficiaries is through the "joint and survivors option." By agreeing to receive a reduced benefit yourself, a qualified retirement amount—usually 50% to 100% of the retiree's benefit—can continue to be paid to the surviving spouse or, occasionally, children. The joint and survivors option is one that should be carefully considered. In most plans, once the retirement benefit begins, *it cannot be changed.*

Consider what would happen to your spouse if, shortly after retiring, you passed away. The company insurance that once covered you has been reduced or eliminated; the retirement benefit would end; and Social Security may or may not be possible for the surviving partner. The way to avoid at least part of this problem is to accept the joint and survivor option, at least the 50% plan, assuring half of your retirement benefit to your spouse for life. When setting up your Retirement Plan, be sure to use the company pension figure which includes a benefit reduction for the joint and survivor option, if you intend to choose it.

C. ANNUITIES AND RETIREMENT INCOME INSURANCE

Typically, these offer a guaranteed annual income for life, often with a joint and survivors option. The income represents both interest and return of your invested capital. However, since they are actuarily calculated, the payment will continue for life, regardless of how long you live. Annuities are an alternative to personal investment, providing safeguards in respect to the sufficiency of your capital. The insurance company, in return for the use of your money, takes the risk of how long you will live.

Other annuities are "period certain" types. In these, payment of benefits is guaranteed for your lifetime, but it is also guaranteed that the payments will last a certain minimum number of years, often 10–20. Should you die before the guaranteed period has elapsed, your designated beneficiary would continue to receive the same benefits until the end of the "period certain."

Retirement income insurance is a combination insurance policy and annuity, providing insurance protection before retirement and an annuity after retirement. In fact, most non-term insurance policies have characteristics that can make them sources of retirement income. (See Chapter 5 discussion of "Sources of 'New' Money" for additional thoughts on this subject.)

Single-premium deferred annuities

A special form of annuity, the single-premium deferred annuity, offers some features that should be considered as alternatives to the types mentioned above. This annuity at the time of this writing, enjoys a special sheltering from federal income taxes. The annuity plan offers guaranteed interest rates for a specific period of time, high interest rates initially, a guaranteed minimum interest rate thereafter, daily interest, compounding and deferral of federal income tax on the interest gained until either the annuity payments begin or the principal and interest are withdrawn from the fund. The plans are offered by insurance companies such as Life Insurance Co. of North America (INA), Nationwide Life Insurance Co., Old Republic Life of New York, Anchor National Life of Phoenix, and Capitol Life of Denver. There are usually front-end commission charges of 4–6% of the investment amount, or, if it is a no-load contract, the charge may be 6–8% of the amount on surrender of the contract.

A typical plan, requiring a minimum single premium of $5–10,000, would guarantee something like:

Minimum Rate	Time Guarantee
7.75%	First year
6.8	Second year
6.0	Third and fourth year
3.5	After the fourth year

You can usually make yearly tax-free partial withdrawals up to your original premium without reporting it as taxable income (according to "First-in, first-out" rule). This tax deferred feature is the biggest advantage of single premium deferred annuities. Some other advantages are:
- Avoiding probate if you should die, since the proceeds in the account go directly to the beneficiary as in any insurance policy.
- Liquidity; since the full annuity value can be claimed at any time prior to the commencement of benefits, subject only to a cancellation fee payable to the insurance company.
- The annuity contract can be used as collateral for a loan.

Tax Tip: If the tax-deferred status of these annuities is *changed* by the Internal Revenue Service, bank savings certificates or municipal bonds might be better financial deals, since you would not have to pay commission charges, or at least not as large charges as those assessed by the insurance companies.

Completing the retirement plan

O.K. We're now ready to make our first cut at a Retirement Plan. The first thing to do is assume a retirement date. This is usually the last day of the month of your 65th birthday for normal retirement, or the last day of the month of your birth for any age down to 55 (or earlier, if applicable). For our example, let's choose early retirement—"Retirement at age 55," take one!

First, find Exhibit II at the end of this chapter, and follow along as we go. (You may find that completing your own Personal Resources Record in the Appendix will be helpful in relating the following example to your own needs.)

Our subject was born in July of 1929 and, therefore, will retire early at the end of July, 1984. In referring to items on the Plan, we'll locate them by column (1–8) and row (1–32). The first entry is under Income—present salary + commissions (column 1, row 1). (Don't worry about cents in this exercise. Nothing is that exact in forecasting.)

INCOME-PRODUCING ASSETS

Next, go down the extreme left-hand column to Assets—Income-Producing (row 20), and list all bonds, stocks, savings accounts, mutual funds, bond funds, income-producing property, etc. If married, both the husband's and wife's assets should be listed. (After all, "The family that retires together, has to live off each other.") Then, go back up to row 2 and go down column 1 putting in the income the corresponding asset brings in that year. For example, spouse's savings of $15,700 at 6¼% (row 26) produces $942 (row 7). It can be seen in the example that, from assets of $159,921, an income of $6720, plus salary has been obtained. That is a return of 4.2% on invested asset value—not a record beater, but we'll get back to that later in Chapter 6, "Smoothing out the Retirement Plan."

TAXABILITY

It will be worthwhile at this time to indicate whether the income produced is taxable under current income tax laws or not. After your entries in column 1, indicate "XT" if the money is exempt from all taxes, "FT" if exempt from federal taxes, and "ST" if exempt from your state's taxes.

FINANCIAL ASSUMPTIONS USED IN PLANNING

Now is the time to review some of the assumptions necessary to make our results meaningful.

1. *Home.* Present home is not included in income-producing assets. Regardless of what you do, you will have to live somewhere. The calculation assumes your present living quarters are as reasonable as anywhere else. (Incidentally, if you don't like any of these assumptions, change them. After all, it's your plan.)
2. *Cost-of-living.* All cost-of-living adjustments are calculated in the Expense Approximater (see Chapter 2).
3. *Salary after retirement.* You do not earn any salary after retirement. If you do, it's "gravy" on the Retirement Plan. It may be that an age 55 Retirement Plan does not show that adequate income for retirement is possible without working. However, it will give you a handle on how much, net, you have to earn while you are retired and for how long.
4. *Legacies.* The plan does not anticipate legacies (although you may do so if you're sure how much they are and when you'll get them), company or Social Security retirement plan improvements (although these are likely), any salary increases (although a final salary figure is assumed in order to price out some benefits), or any special retirement incentives (unless you are sure of date and amount).
5. *Interest calculations.* These are based on tables in the Appendix. For plans of 6 or fewer years, use the percentages that show daily compounding (Table A); for plans longer than 6 years, use the one-dollar compounded tables, which compound annually only (Tables B and C). This is a known inherent error on the conservative side and is intended to help offset interest rate fluctuations over time.

ESTIMATING FINAL SALARY

Here are some rules of thumb for guessing final salary. Increase your present salary 1% for each year up to retirement if 10 or fewer years to go; 3% per year if 15 or fewer years to go; and 5% per year if 20 or fewer years to go. In our sample, it's 9 years, increasing salary to about $40,000, which you would post in column 2, row 1. In the target retirement year, our employee works 7 months of the 12, or 7/12 of $40,000, earning $23,333, which is entered in column 3, row 1. Of course, after retirement, we are assuming no salary, so column 4, row 1, is zero, as are all subsequent columns on this row.

Moving back down to Assets (below row 20), municipal bonds remain the same, although one bond does mature, and it is "rolled over" into a bond with a slightly better return (hence the improvement in income on row 2). The municipal bond fund (row 22) has grown apace as the bond dividends are reinvested, and it has now produced tax-free income of its own (row 3). (Example from appendix Table C: 6% for 8 years = 10.49 x $2257 = $23675; 9 years = 12.18 x $2257 = $27490.) The annual dividend on company stock (row 23) and the market price of the stock are assumed to be unchanged across the board (row 4). However, the number of shares has increased because of a stock purchase plan. Then, the first full year after retirement, when the impact of a tax on the capital gain will be less, the stock will be sold in 25% increments over 4 years and the proceeds reinvested in a municipal bond fund at 6% (rows 11 and 30).

The certificates of deposit (Row 24) and savings accounts (rows 25 and 26) increase is calculated by Table B in the Appendix, assuming no additional deposits are made in them. The same is true for mutual funds (row 28) and miscellaneous (row 29). (Example from Appendix Table B: 6% for 8 years = 1.59 x $16900 = $26871; 6% for 9 years = 1.69 x $16900 = $28561.)

E bonds (row 27) can be priced annually. Ask your local bank or savings and loan association to save you the December U.S. Savings Bonds—Series E—Redemption Values by Denomination charts. E bonds do not pay out interest; instead, they increase in face value. So in the retirement year, you may convert them to H bonds, which do pay out interest. This will not be a taxable exchange, yet it will convert the bonds to income sources. When the H bonds are finally cashed in years later, the interest gain that was always deferred on the E bonds will become payable in the tax year in which the H bonds are surrendered. Although H bonds pay 6% interest, the first two semi-annual payments will be less than that, the rest slightly more. For our purposes, a flat interest rate is assumed. Another advantage of H bonds is their exemption from state or local taxes, since federal obligations cannot be taxed by other than federal taxing authorities. So E bonds have special values in your capital building portfolio—deferred, sheltered gain, state tax-sheltered income after conversion to H bonds, and, since bond-buying campaigns seem increasingly considered as corporate "good citizen" responsibilities, some "brownie" points for your company and you.

CAPITAL GAINS, DIVIDENDS, CERTIFICATES OF DEPOSIT, E BONDS, AND H BONDS

PERSONAL RESOURCES ASSETS

By the Target Retirement Year, you will have "locked in" your Personal resources assets. In our example, the $159,921 of assets from column 1 grows to $250,456 in column 3, the retirement year. The return of $13,049 from column 4, row 12, is 5.21% now, a little more respectable. In fact, the strategy in this sample of selling off stock and converting to higher paying investments will, within a few years, increase the return on investment of the assets to over 6%, much of it tax free.

COMPANY RETIREMENT BENEFITS

The next calculation is your company retirement. Many companies publish updates or status reports on benefits. If yours is one of these, you've got a head start in figuring it out. Many other companies publish their retirement formula in "Employee Benefits" books, from which you'll have to dig out the information. Don't be discouraged at the unbelievably complicated formulas. Just get ahold of your old tax-record W-2's, which have company earnings reported, apply the formulas, and work it out. In our sample, after 50% "joint and survivors" is applied, our subject's annual company retirement income is $10,445 (column 4, row 13). Apply 5/12 of this ($4,352) in the target year, (column 3, row 13) and all of it thereafter. Since this was a non-contributory plan, all of it is taxable.

SOCIAL SECURITY BENEFITS

Next come Social Security benefits. In our example, since retirement is calculated for age 55, Social Security won't apply for 7 years. (You can use the charts shown earlier in this chapter to approximate your own Social Security benefits.)

TOTALING UP

Now, add up the columns to sum the total income (row 16), and how much of that income is federally taxable (row 17). Obviously, when doing your own retirement plan, you would produce a column for every year (to be inserted in place of our blank "column 5") until your income becomes fixed; in our example, it would take 15 columns. Note that taxable capital gains (row 18) are not included in total income (row 16), nor in taxable income (row 17). These are one-time tax liabilities that occur when an asset is converted, or a deferred tax is reported for tax purposes (H bond redemption), or a sheltered income source is converted (IRA or Keogh). Although tax must be paid, do not confuse your Retirement Plan by merging the dollars into annual income for retirement. In our example, the capital gain on each of 68 shares sold is about $100 per share, or, $6800. Half of that is taxed as long term capital gain, hence the $3400 taxable for each of 4 years.

As a final step in our example, we post Total Income (row 16) to the Expense Approximater in Chapter 2 (Exhibit I) on the Annual Income line for the appropriate year.

You now have completed the "first cut" and would be ready to match income to expenses, except that you first have to calculate taxes for the Expense Approximator. Chapter 4 shows you how to do that.

EXHIBIT II. **RETIREMENT PLAN (Sample) — FIRST CUT (Early Retirement, Age 55).**

		Now	Last Full Yr. Before Retirement	Target Retirement Year	1st Full Year After Retirement	Husband Soc. Sec. Full	Fixed Income; Wife Soc. Sec.
INCOME	Year: Age:	1976 47	1983 54	1984 55	1985 56	1992 63	1996 67
Salary & Commissions		36500	40000	23333	0	0	0
Municipal Bonds - 6.1%		2257xt	2372xt	2372xt	2372xt	2635xt	2745xt
Municipal Bond Fund - 6%		0	1420ft	1649ft	1649ft	1649ft	1649ft
Company Stock - $7 Dividend		1330	1820	1890	1414	0	0
No. 1 Sav. & Loan Co. - 8%		800	1303	1326	1326	1326	1326
No. 2 Sav. & Loan Co. - 6%		1014	1610	1712	1712	1712	1712
Spouse Savings - 6¼%		942	1599	1687	1687	1687	1687
E Bonds - 6%		0	0	Conv to H Bonds	1031st	1031st	1031st
Mutual Fund Dividend - 7%		377	644	690	690	690	690
Misc. Assets - 5¼%		0	162	162	162	162	162
Savings From Stock Sale - 6%		0	0	0	1006ft	4050ft	4050ft
*Personal Resources Income		43220	50930	34821	13049	14942	15052
Company Retirement		0	0	4352	10445	10445	10445
Social Security		0	0	0	0	4368xt	6552xt
*Total Income		43220	50930	39173	23494	29755	32049
*Taxable Income (Federal)		40963	47138	35152	18467	17053	17053
Taxable Capital Gains		0	0	0	3400	0	0
ASSETS — INCOME-PRODUCING							
Municipal Bonds - 6.1%		50000	50000	50000	50000	50000	50000
Muni. Bond Fund - 6%		2257	23675	27490	27490	27490	27490
Company Stock		47500	65000	67500	50625	0	0
No. 1 Sav. & Loan Co. -8%		10000	18392	19744	19744	19744	19744
No. 2 Sav. & Loan Co. - 6%		16900	26871	28561	28561	28561	28561
Spouse Savings - 6¼%		15700	25591	27004	27004	27004	27004
E Bonds - 6%		10177	16181	17199	17199	17199	17199
Mutual Fund - 7%		5387	9211	9858	9858	9858	9858
Misc. Assets - 5¼%		2000	2960	3100	3100	3100	3100
Savings From Stock Sale - 6%		0	0	0	16875	67500	67500
* Total Assets		159921	237881	250456	250456	250456	250456

MAJOR EVENTS

4. Using the tax estimater

While working on the Expense Approximater in Chapter 2 (Exhibit I), you found you couldn't complete the income tax portion of the form, primarily because you had not yet calculated taxable income. That required working out the "First Cut at the Retirement Plan" (Exhibit II) in Chapter 3. You should now be ready to finish the tax portion of the Expense Approximater, and see if your income will cover your outlays.

Using the Tax Estimater form in the Appendix (an example of which appears at the end of this chapter), select the years you've already examined for expenses and work on these years for determining taxes. In our continuing example, these would be 1985, 1994 and 1998. The federal income tax portion should be applicable to all readers of this book. However, the state and county income tax portion will only apply to residents of states in which you pay such taxes. Our example happens to be for the state of Maryland. You'll have to work out some handy system for your own state, since there are too many possibilities to consider effectively within the scope of this book.

Picking up income data and determining deductions, taxable income, and tax rate

Follow along on our Tax Estimater Sample (Exhibit III). Picking up income data directly from our exemplary Retirement Plan (Exhibit II), let's fill in the appropriate categories of income on the tax estimater. Then, depending on how good a handle you have on expenses, proceed to estimate rental expenses, itemized deductions, and so forth. If you can't estimate itemized deductions too well, use 16% as a working figure. The years that were selected include the year the husband reaches 65 (1994) and the year his spouse reaches 65 (1998), for in those years their dependency exemption increases. Notice that income exempt from federal income tax is not included in this exhibit.

After calculating (A) Taxable income, subtract (B) total deductions from it. The result is income subject to tax. With this figure, go to Table V, where the tax rates in effect at the time of this publication are listed. Three classes of taxpayer are included in Table V:
- Single individuals
- Unmarried heads of households
- Married, filing joint return

TABLE V. **FEDERAL INCOME TAX RATES (effective in 1977).**

Single Individual		Unmarried Head of Household		Married Joint Return		% on excess over Taxable Income
Taxable Income	**Tax Payable**	**Taxable Income**	**Tax Payable**	**Taxable Income**	**Tax Payable**	
$ 500	$ 70			$ 1000	$ 140	15%
1000	145	$ 1000	$ 140	2000	290	16
1500	225			3000	450	17
		2000	300			18
2000	310	4000	660	4000	620	19
4000	690					21
		6000	1040	8000	1380	22
		8000	1480			23
6000	1110					24
8000	1590	10000	1940	12000	2260	25
10000	2090	12000	2440			27
		14000	2980	16000	3260	28
12000	2630					29
14000	3210	16000	3540			31
		18000	4160	20000	4380	32
16000	3830					34
		20000	4800			35
18000	4510	22000	5500	24000	5660	36
20000	5230	24000	6220			38
				28000	7100	39
22000	5990					40
		26000	6980			41
		28000	7800	32000	8660	42
26000	7590	32000	9480	36000	10340	45
		36000	11280	40000	12140	48
32000	10290			44000	14060	50
		38000	12240			51
		40000	13260			52
				52000	18060	53
38000	13290	44000	15340	64000	24420	55
		50000	18640			56
		52000	19760	76000	31020	58
		64000	26720			59
44000	16590			88000	37980	60
		70000	30260			61
50000	20190	76000	33920	100000	45180	62
		80000	36400			63
60000	26390	88000	41440	120000	57580	64
70000	32790	100000	49120	140000	70380	66
		120000	62320			67
80000	39390	140000	75720	160000	83580	68
90000	46190	160000	89320	180000	97180	69
100000	53090	180000	103120	200000	110980	70

Calculating federal income tax

In Exhibit III, our subject is married, filing a joint return with an income subject to tax in 1985 of $16,668. Looking at Table V for that category, we find the tax on $16,668 is $3260 plus 28% of every dollar over $16,000 or $187.04. The total is $3,447, which is posted to the Tax Estimater (Exhibit III). Notice that this calculation includes tax paid on capital gain. If the capital gain had not occurred, taxable income would be reduced to $18,467. Assuming the same tax deductions as before, "income subject to tax" would drop to $13,990. In the same tax category, tax on that amount is $2260 plus 25% of all amounts over $12,000, or $497.50. The total is $2757. The net tax cost of selling ¼ of our subject's stock holdings is $690. Considering the capital gain was $6800, the effective tax on the profit is only 10.1%

The same technique is used for succeeding years. See if you can reach the same tax dollar figures by using Table V for 1994 and 1998 on the Tax Estimater. Post these federal tax dollars to the Expense Approximater (Exhibit I).

Calculating state income tax

The state income tax calculation, as has been mentioned, will vary widely. Without going into great detail for our exemplary Maryland tax, Federal tax form figures are used. The dividend exclusion is not allowed and state income tax itemized in deductions would be added back. At the same time, income from federal obligations is excluded. The tax is narrowly graduated to 5%, with a piggy-bank county tax—50% of the state tax—tied in. This makes the effective rate 7½%. The resulting tax for each year is posted to the Expense Approximater (Exhibit I), and, finally, that form can be completed.

Finishing up the expense approximater

Referring back to Exhibit I, the Expense Approximater, it is now possible to total the expenses for our selected years. Remember that "annual income" from Exhibit II, the Retirement Plan, has already been posted in "annual income" on the Expense Approximater. Now, subtract "total expenses" from "annual income" to calculate the long- or short-fall. In this case, there is a short-fall the first year of $188, changing to a long-fall of $12,340 in the later years when income becomes fixed, except for possible cost-of-living adjustments of Social Security or company retirement benefits.

An interesting observation is that the early years of retirement, especially of early retirement, are the toughest financially. Assets begin to be more productive, Social Security and spouse's Social Security start, and things get better as you get older. In our example, substantial surpluses exist in the later years either for reinvestment to produce even more income, or to account for underestimates in expenses, or for a super wing-ding each year! Further to the point, in early retirement, when income most needs augmenting, the early retiree is often still young enough to compete in the full- or part-time job market. However, this is not typical. Most people planning their own retirement will find a substantial short-fall in the early retirement years and, perhaps, a break-even in later years. This sober reflection leads us to the following chapters on finding ways to increase assets and, ultimately, personal income and money for children's education.

EXHIBIT III. **TAX ESTIMATER (Sample).**

	Year: 1985	1994	1998
	Age: 56	65	69
Federal Income Tax			
Salary	0	0	0
Private Pension (Company Plan)	10,445	10,445	10,445
Rental Income	0	0	0
Dividends (Taxable)	2,104	690	690
Interest (Taxable)	5,918	5,918	5,918
Capital Gains (Net Taxable)	3,400	0	0
(A) Taxable Income	21,867	17,053	17,053
Less deductions:			
Rental expenses (Tax, Insurance)	0	0	0
Itemized Deductions (or 16%)	3,499	2,728	2,728
Dividend Exclusion	200	200	200
Dependent Exemptions ($750 × Number)	(2) 1,500	(3) 2,250	(4) 3,000
(B) Total Deductions	5,199	5,178	5,928
Income Subject to Tax (A−B)	16,668	11,875	11,125
Tax (from Current IRS Tables)	3,447	2,234	2,067
State and County Income Tax (Md.)			
Taxable Income (Federal)	21,867	17,053	17,053
Additions	+ 200	+ 200	+ 200
Subtractions	− 1,031	− 1,031	− 1,031
Itemized Deductions	− 3,499	− 2,728	− 2,728
Dependent Exemptions ($800 × Number)	(2) − 1,600	(3) − 2,400	(4) − 3,200
Net Taxable Income	15,937	11,094	10,294
Tax on First $3000	135	135	135
Plus 7½% of Remainder	970	607	547
Total State and County Tax	1,105	742	682

5. Now, let's get serious!

Okay! You've gone through the first cut at a Retirement Plan and have found either you will make it financially at retirement—or you won't. What can you do to brighten your retirement prospects?

Prioritizing needs

First, you can get serious about your priorities. You can arrange your needs into three categories:
- Necessary and mandatory
- Desirable
- Nice to have

What's necessary and mandatory? You have to feed, clothe, shelter, and transport yourself and your family; you have to get your children educated; you have to assure the health of your family. There's no way around these requirements. And what's more, everything has a priority. For example—

Transportation:
- Necessary and mandatory (take a bus, car pool, ride a bike, walk)
- Desirable (economy car, motor scooter, mo-ped)
- Nice to have (Lincoln, Rolls Royce, Jaguar, private airplane)

Educate children:
- Necessary and mandatory (complete high school)
- Desirable (attend) trade school, 4-year public college)
- Nice to have (private college, 4-year education)

Housing:
- Necessary and mandatory (apartment, trailer home, condominium)
- Desirable (small townhouse, two-family house)
- Nice to have (private home, luxury apartment, summer cottage)

You have the idea now? Everything can be prioritized, and how you do that is a function of your lifestyle, income, peer pressure, family pressure, cultural background, and, as far as this book is concerned, your needs at retirement. A personal assessment of this "chitlins-hamburger-steak" philosophy is something you have to work out for yourself.

TRADE-OFFS

There are trade-offs, of course. You can trade the cost of maintaining two cars for an annual, super vacation, or a big house in the suburbs for fur coats and diamond rings.

There used to be a quotation that said, "The two biggest investments you can make in your lifetime are a house and a car, as long as you have your health." Well, current economic conditions have changed that expression. Good health could be your most disastrous expense. Today, with health insurance, HMO's (Health maintenance organizations), and major medical insurance, catastrophic health costs can be avoided, although the expenses for premiums for such insurance are not modest. Therefore, these expenses have climbed to the "necessary and mandatory" position on your priority list.

Speaking of trade-offs, replacing that "car" on the list and, in some areas of the country, that "house," is equivalent to the cost of a college education. That leads us to the next section of this chapter—"Stashing It Away for College," since our first cut at the Retirement Plan did not really take that expense into full consideration.

A. Stashing It Away for College

WHAT A COLLEGE EDUCATION WILL COST

Back in the early 1950s, the tuition at a four-year Ivy League university was $2400 for all four years. Today, 25 years later, that amount would hardly cover one semester's tuition at the same school, an eightfold increase. That increase represents a 32% average increase per year, or about an 8.7% increase compounded over 25 years. College costs continue to rise at about an 8% compounded rate per year. In the face of these facts how can you afford to pay for your children's education?

College costs are projected through time assuming a continuation of the 8% compounded growth rate in the average college cost calculator, Exhibit IV, which you will find at the end of this section. Tuition, room, board, and fees are estimated on a semester basis. To figure what a college education will cost during any four-year period, start with the first projected semester and count down 8 semesters. For example, for a student starting in the fall of 1979, the college cost will total $21,710 for the average private college or $11,340 for the average public college by the spring of 1983, when the student graduates. This is a figure for one student. You would simply calculate the same way for each child to be financed through college.

PUT ASIDE BEFORE COLLEGE STARTS

Now, if you had all the money *in one lump sum* at the start of your child's college experience, you could be receiving interest on the unused balance. A *base*, representing a declining amount of dollars at 6% interest for four years, is also indicated on Exhibit IV. In our example, only $19,430 would be needed to pay for $21,710 worth of average private college costs and $10,200 instead of $11,340 for the average public college starting in 1979—a reduction of 10% under out-of-pocket costs.

So, "Lesson 1" is: If you put aside the money *before* college starts, rather than pay for it as your child progresses from semester to semester, your out-of-pocket college costs are decreased.

By saving early, you can reduce these costs even more through the magic of compound interest. If you put aside a college fund at the start of your child's entry into high school, four years earlier, then the cash requirements for college would be $15,420 for a private college and $8095 for a public college, a reduction of nearly 30% under out-of-pocket college costs. These figures can be easily calculated by dividing the appropriate compounded amount of "one dollar" from Table B (in the Appendix) into the "base" indicated in Exhibit IV. In our example, using 6% for four years, we get 1.26 as the divisor from Appendix Table B, which we divide into the bases of $19,430 and $10,200, giving $15,420 and $8095 respectively. If you began saving at the end of your child's grammar school, six years before college started, only $13,683 and $7183 would have been needed, a reduction of 37% under out-of-pocket costs.

"Wait a minute," you say. "How about taxes on the interest? Won't they reduce the amount you have available to spend for college?"

UNIFORM GIFTS TO MINORS

That's the beauty of stashing it away for college. You can have the government "pay" part of the tuition by eliminating taxes on your savings interest. The way to do this is to transfer the income-producing asset from your own funds to the child's under the Uniform Gifts to Minors Act (UGTMA). Since the child's income from interest alone will be less than taxable minimums or, at worst, will be taxable at minimal rates, there is a substantial savings over the 28%, 32%, 39%, and so forth, that you are paying in taxes on your own top income.

Further, you can give gifts of securities to your child as well as cash. The limits without gift tax implications are $3000 per year per child ($6000 if your spouse concurs). In this way, although the cost basis of the security is calculated for the child in the same way as for the donor, any capital gain you may have earned on the security will be paid by the custodian for the child when the security is sold. There are no tax consequences to the donor on any gain prior to the date of the gift. For example, assume that you bought 100 shares of stock three years ago for $100 per share. That stock increases in value to $154 per share today. Instead of selling it and giving the proceeds to your child to pay for college, give the child the stock instead, within the gift limits, letting the child sell it. The cost basis for the child would be $100 per share. You would not be taxed on any of the gain. If the child sold it for $154 per share (excluding commission), the child would have $15,400, enough to pay for the $21,710 worth of college in our example above—and all it cost you was $10,000! The tax on the long term capital gain of $2700 (½ of $5400) would be paid at *the lower tax rates applicable to the child*, if any tax applies at all, since the gift and sale would usually be spread over several years.

Convinced? OK, let's talk a little about "uniform gifts to minors" acts. First of all, every jurisdiction has an act of one sort or another—differing somewhat in phraseology and definition of the "age of majority." They do have these aspects in common:

1. A gift under the law is a complete, irrevocable donation where the donor gives up all rights to the property.
2. The gift vests title in the minor, which may not be revoked by the donor under any circumstances.
3. Registration of securities is in the name of an adult custodian who is obliged to use the property solely for the benefit of the minor and not for himself.

The kinds of gifts allowed, depending on the state, include money, mutual fund shares, life insurance policies, annuity contracts, and securities. Even though the property must be used solely for the minor's benefit, not all the benefits of giving securities accrue to the minor alone. Your *own* benefits may include the following privileges.

Tax Benefits to donors

A. Federal Income Tax
- Shift income from higher to lower tax brackets.
- Parents of the minor continue to receive the $750 exemption for each child under 19 years of age or a full time student if they provide more than half the child's support.
- Child gets his or her own $750 exemption.
- No capital gains tax is assessed until the security is sold, and then only on the difference between the donor's cost basis and the price on the date of sale.

B. State Income Tax
- States generally follow federal rules on who is taxable.

45

C. Federal Gift and Estate Tax
- Donor may give away $3000 per year without tax penalty to each donee.
- If the donor is married and his or her spouse agrees to the gift, up to $6000 per year can be given without tax liability.
- Gifts are valued at the time of the gift at fair market value. The gift is considered completed at the time of transfer so that a change of custodian (joint custodians are not authorized) or end of the custodianship when the child reaches majority is not treated as a gift.

Some qualifications should be noted, however. The IRS claims gifts under the Uniform Gifts to Minors Act are taxable in the estate of a donor who is also custodian. Therefore, it would be wiser to appoint the spouse as custodian, or person other than the donor. Further, each gift must be to a single minor; you cannot have two or more minors considered jointly as one donee. Finally, although gifts greater than $3000 per year are legal and possible, an amount over $3000 would be counted as part of the estate of the donor, and may require payment of gift tax. (See Appendix, Table D.)

The procedure for setting up Uniform Gifts to Minors accounts is simple. However, you are best advised to consult your securities broker, attorney, or tax advisor, since regulations change from time to time, and this book in no way purports itself to offer legal, tax-law, or expert technical advice. The information presented here is not exhaustive, but merely representative of the advantages that may result from implementation of the Uniform Gifts to Minors Act.

The ages of majority under the UGTMA vary considerably since many states have recently revised majority statutes because of constitutional voting-age reductions. As of this writing, the UGTMA ages of majority were:

Age 21 — Men and Women

Alabama	Illinois	Massachusetts	New Mexico	Rhode Island
Canal Zone	Indiana	Minnesota	New York	South Carolina
Colorado	Iowa	Mississippi	North Dakota	Texas
District of Columbia	Kentucky	Missouri	Ohio	Utah
Florida	Louisiana	Nevada	Oklahoma	Virgin Islands
Hawaii	Maryland	New Hampshire	Oregon	Virginia
				Wyoming

Age 20 — Men and Women

Nebraska

Age 19 — Men and Women

Alaska

Age 18 — Men and Women

Arizona	Georgia	Michigan	Pennsylvania	Washington
California	Idaho	Montana	South Dakota	West Virginia
Connecticut	Kansas	New Jersey	Tennessee	Wisconsin
Delaware	Maine	North Carolina	Vermont	

Age 21 — Men; Age 18 — Women

Arkansas

Regardless of the date of majority, the benefits of establishing a college fund using the UGTMA are still great. Clearly, to achieve all the benefits, the fund should be established while your child is still a minor. However, annual gifts of $3000 may be given to any person, minor or not, without tax consequences. Some other things to be done include:

- Obtaining a Social Security number for the minor. Since all income will be for the benefit of the minor, the custodian for that minor would file a tax return under the child's own number.
- Appointment of a custodian. No bond is required if the custodian is not being compensated for services. The custodian should keep detailed records of the custodianship, since he or she may be required to give an accounting at any time if the minor, child at majority, parents, or successors petition for one.

Nice? "Lesson 2," then, is: If you put money aside for college, put it aside *completely*. Further, *give it to the child* whose benefit you wish to assure, preferably under the Uniform Gifts to Minors Act, and let the government help pay for your children's education.

Suppose, however, that you want to give the money to your child, but can't do it all at once. Fine. Up to $3000 ($6000 if your spouse agrees) per child per year means that within 2 days you could give up to $12,000 per child: $3000 + $3000 on December 31 and $3000 + $3000 on January 1. Or you can spread it out over years. Remember that the *sooner* you give the income-producing asset to your child, the sooner you shelter that income from tax, or minimize the tax.

THE FIRST FINANCIAL PLAN: PROVIDING EDUCATION FOR YOUR CHILDREN

This leads to "lesson 3": The first financial plan to set up is one to finance the education of your children. Set it and forget it.

Of course, there may be other ways to help finance your child's education, including any or all of the following:
- Child's earnings
- Scholarships
- Student aid
- Student loans

However, the only *sure* way is to plan to finance it through your own resources. The gift approach makes this possible and costs are relatively low if the approach is begun early enough.

That puts the children's education out of the way. However, in the process, you may have used up many of the income-producing assets that you used in Chapter 3 to take your first cut at a Retirement Plan. If you haven't waited too long, it is still possible to recoup; clearly, the longer you wait to set up the kids' education funds, the more you'll require out-of-pocket expenditures. (See Exhibit IV, p. 51.). If there was no short-fall on the first cut at the Retirement Plan, there probably is now. In any case, what you need is a successful way to stash away money for yourself.

B. Stashing It Away for Yourself

The merits of thrift and a regular plan for saving as a discipline were discussed in Chapter 2. In this chapter we will discuss some saving gambits and some unexpected sources of "new" money. One saving trick was mentioned in Chapter 2—the trick of pretending FICA deductions go on for the full year and depositing the excess for your own benefit. Some of the saving gambits that we'll investigate may not sound like much, but everything adds up.

11 SAVING TRICKS

1. *FICA deductions assumed for the full year.* (See Chapter 2.)

This was a much better saving trick before the latest Social Security Law was passed in December of 1977. Because the maximum amount of Social Security earnings was raised, Social Security payroll deductions will continue longer and longer into the year. Similarly, the amount of the Social Security deduction will be larger and larger due to both higher percentage rates and also higher eligible income. As a practical matter, this savings trick will be over for possible savers on the following schedule:

Gross Earned Income	Year	Annual Soc. Sec. Deduct.	Month Soc. Sec. Deduction ends	Amount you save each month/total for year	
$15,000	1978	$ 907.50	Never	None	None
$20,000	1978	$1070.85	November	$100.83	$ 139.15
	1979	1226.00	Never	None	None
$25,000	1978	$1070.85	September	$126.04	$ 441.65
	1979	1403.77	November	127.71	128.73
	1980	1532.50	Never	None	None
$30,000	1978	$1070.85	August	$151.25	$ 744.15
	1979	1403.77	October	153.25	435.23
	1980	1587.67	November	153.25	251.33
	1981	1975.05	December	166.25	19.95
	1982	2010.00	Never	None	None
$35,000	1978	$1070.85	July	$176.46	$1046.65
	1979	1403.77	August	178.79	741.73
	1980	1587.67	September	178.79	557.83
	1981	1975.05	November	193.96	352.45
	1982	2130.60	November	195.42	214.40
	1983	2271.30	December	195.42	73.70
	1984	2345.00	Never	None	None
$40,000	1978	$1070.85	June	$201.67	$1349.15
	1979	1403.77	July	204.33	1048.23
	1980	1587.67	August	204.33	864.33
	1981	1975.05	September	221.67	684.95
	1982	2130.60	October	223.33	549.40
	1983	2271.30	November	223.33	408.70
	1984	2412.00	November	223.33	268.00
	1985	2686.05	December	235.00	133.95
	1986	2860.00	Never	None	None
$45,000	1978	$1070.85	May	$226.88	$1651.65
	1979	1403.77	July	229.88	1354.73
	1980	1587.67	July	229.88	1170.83
	1981	1975.05	August	249.38	1017.45
	1982	2130.60	September	251.25	884.40
	1983	2271.30	October	251.25	743.70
	1984	2412.00	October	251.25	603.00
	1985	2686.05	November	264.38	486.45
	1986	2874.30	November	268.13	343.20
	1987 on	3045.90	December	268.13	171.60

It is interesting to note that Joe Average Taxpayer, with a wife and two children, earned $16,500. The earned income subject to Social Security Taxes has now reached past the point of median income in the U.S. See Table I in Chapter 3 for the schedule of eligible earnings increases.

2. *Loose change.* Place a mason jar or a small piggy bank on your dresser or night table. Toss in all your loose change every night. Once a month deposit it in your savings account. If you save 75 cents per working day, that's $180 per year, which, in 10 years at 6% interest, will grow to over $2514. (See Table C in the Appendix.)

3. *Expense accounts.* If you work for a company that reimburses you for business travel, deposit the reimbursement checks in a savings account. If you cash them, you'll probably spend the money.

4. *Credit Unions.* If your company has a credit union, there are usually three advantages to utilizing it:
- They pay as high, if not higher, interest rates as savings and loan associations.
- They are a source of relatively low-interest borrowing.
- They will accept regular payroll deductions for deposit. In this way, you can deduct 5%, 6%, 10%, or whatever you like from your salary as a regular, disciplined savings. 10% of a $20,000 salary each year will grow to $53,780 at 7% credit-union interest in 15 years. (From Table C in the Appendix.)

5. *Employee stock purchase plans.* Even if you do not like stocks as a medium for long-term capital growth, you owe it to yourself to investigate any such plan your company may have. Usually, stock is sold to the employee at a discount, or shares purchased are matched by the company, or some other such incentive is created to encourage employees to buy shares through payroll deductions. You can sell these shares immediately, if you wish, to "lock in" the discount. Or, you can transfer them, under the Uniform Gifts to Minors Act, so your children can sell them later to cover their college expenses. Of course, if yours is a "growth company," you may just wish to hold the shares as a speculation for growth. Again, consider the "rule of 72" in determining whether to sell or hold. If you can assure yourself, beyond a reasonable doubt, that your stock will better than double in, say, 10 years, then it would be to your advantage to hold it rather than sell it. As part of your determination, remember the tax-saving advantages of long term capital gains on the profit. If you received 7.2% interest on your money, which would then double in 10 years, the taxes on the profit would be at your highest tax rate.

6. *Interest on demand deposits.* Except for the six New England states, it is illegal for banks to pay interest on checking accounts. However, there is an easy way around the restriction. Look for a full-service bank in your area that gives day-of-deposit, day-of-withdrawal savings account interest, often at 5%. After finding such a bank, make all of your deposits from salary or other sources into this savings account

EXHIBIT IV. AVERAGE COLLEGE COST CALCULATOR.*

Start Year	Tuition, room, board + fees Public	Private	4 year requirement Public	Private	Base Public	Base Private
1975F	$ 925	$1771				
1976S	925	1771				
1976F	999	1912				
1977S	999	1912				
1977F	1079	2065				
1978S	1079	2065				
1978F	1165	2230				
1979S	1165	2230	$ 8336	$15956	$ 7500	$14280
1979F	1258	2409				
1980S	1258	2409	9002	17232	8050	15480
1980F	1359	2602				
1981S	1359	2602	9722	18612	8700	16880
1981F	1468	2810				
1982S	1468	2810	10500	20102	9450	17980
1982F	1585	3034				
1983S	1585	3034	11340	21710	10200	19430
1983F	1712	3277				
1984S	1712	3277	12248	23446	11000	20980
1984F	1849	3540				
1985S	1849	3540	13228	25322	11850	22680
1985F	1997	3823				
1986S	1997	3823	14286	27348	12800	24480
1986F	2156	4128				
1987S	2156	4128	15428	29536	13800	26430
1987F	2329	4458				
1988S	2329	4458	16662	31898	14900	28580
1988F	2515	4816				
1989S	2515	4816	17994	34450	16100	30900
1989F	2717	5201				
1990S	2717	5201	19434	37206	17400	33350
1990F	2933	5616				
1991S	2933	5616	20988	40182	18800	36000
1991F	3169	6065				
1992S	3169	6065	22668	43396	20300	38900
1992F	3422	6552				
1993S	3422	6552	24482	46868	21900	41970
1993F	3696	7076				
1994S	3696	7076	26440	50618	23650	45340

*Assumes 8% Tuition cost increase per year and a declining base for four years at 6% interest.
Source: The College Scholarship Service, 1975.

instead of your checking account. Then instruct the bank to transfer some specific amount of dollars, say $200, to your checking account in that same bank, every week. If you maintain a modest balance in your savings account, $200–300 generally, the bank offers free checking. This means that you are collecting 5% interest on money that will be used in your checking account to pay current, everyday bills. If you need more transferred to checking, just inform the bank and it will be done that instant. If you are accustomed to maintaining a $1000 checking account balance on the average (as can be seen from Appendix Table A), that would result in about $52 extra in interest each year. No big deal you say? $52 a year at 6% interest for 15 years results in $1282—money you will never see if you continue to keep your checking account funds in a plain checking account, where the bank gets to keep the interest! (Use Appendix Table C for these calculations.)

7. *Taking advantage of billing cycles.* Every bill you receive is, in a way, a saving trick. Let's say your utility bills are due 20 days after receipt. Do you pay them as received or do you wait the 20 days? If you pay them right away, you are losing the 5% per year available to you through "trick #6" for 20 extra days. If, for example, your annual electric bill is $600, averaging $50 per month, and you can delay paying the bill for 20 days without penalty each month, you are in effect, collecting interest on $50 for 20 days and you do this 12 times each year. The mathematics look like this.

A = 5% annual interest rate = .0001369863 interest rate per day

B = 20 days delay times 12 months = 240 delay days

C = amount due per month = $50

D = Savings = A × B × C = $1.64

So what, you say—$1.64 won't ensure my retirement. Yet if you use the same legal delay tactics for *all* your bills, say $1000 worth per month, you gain $32.80 for the year. At 6% for 15 years, that's another $809 you wouldn't have otherwise. (Incidentally, credit card purchases work even harder for you since the time between purchase and date the money is due is often 50 days to 3 months.) You might say that the trick of delaying payments to the last possible moment, results in a "discount for delay" over 3¼% per year!

8. *E bond purchases through payroll savings.* A few dollars per week can add up to a tidy amount over several years with the advantage of sheltering income growth—that is, no taxes until cashed in. A payroll deduction of $6.25 per month will buy you four $25 E bonds each year.

This is also a way to build up college money for your children. Just have the bonds taken out in their names and, not only will the growth be sheltered, but the interest will be virtually tax-free when the bond is cashed in by the child. Interest on federal obligations is exempt from state income taxes, too. It is to your advantage to purchase new bonds as quickly as possible in order to start the interest going; therefore, buy in low denominations—$25 or $50 bond.

9. *Money market funds.* Many mutual funds offer no-load, liquid asset accounts which are invested in short-term, commercial "paper," such as promissory notes, bankers' acceptances, and certificates of deposit. The "no-load" mutual fund earns its money from a management fee rather than by charging a commission for buying or selling. These funds reflect the interest rates on the market more accurately than do savings accounts. These funds are closely regulated, and have paid as high as 12% interest in the mid-1970s. The advantages to the investor are several:

- Interest rate fluctuations accurately reflect the money market.
- They are liquid; many funds allow you to write checks on your investment to pay large bills (usually over $500); the fund automatically cashes enough of your shares to cover the check.
- The fund is constantly managed, allowing maximum return.
- The risk is spread over many industries and institutions.
- Minimum investment is $1000—$2500, substantially less than it would be were you to negotiate your own purchases (where the minimum investment is often $100,000 or more).
- You can generally invest additional funds, after the initial investment, of $100 or more.
- Automatic reinvestment of daily interest is assured.

The disadvantages are:

- The interest rates go down as rapidly as they go up (paying about 5¾% in late 1976, for example).
- The money is not insured by any federal agency.
- You generally have to find the funds that offer these services on your own, since stock brokers do not get involved in funds for which they do not receive commission. (See Chapter 9 for the names of some of these funds.)
- The interest is fully taxable as ordinary income.

10. *Municipal bond funds.* One variation of the money market fund is a relatively new development called the municipal bond fund, which can

pass tax-exempt income on to investors. These funds work virtually the same way as the money-market fund, that is, no-load front or back, and with these *additional* advantages:

- Income will be of three types:

(1) Federal tax-free income on municipal bonds; (2) short-term taxable income on money waiting to buy municipals; and (3) capital gains (or losses) on bonds sold during the management of the fund.

- Bonds will be of generally high quality, although not insured.
- Income will be reinvested to buy more tax-free holdings.
- Some require as low as a $100 minimum investment to start, with $25 minimum additional investments allowable thereafter.

You can be your own money manager by having accounts in both types of funds—municipal bond and money market. If they are invested with the same firm, you can move the money back and forth between them to promptly take advantage of rising interest rates in the money market account, or to stabilize your investment with the municipal bond account when interest rates drop. (See "Sources of New Money" in this chapter, particularly Table VII showing the effect of tax-free income on return, and Chapter 9 for names of no-load municipal bond funds.)

11. *Withholding Tax.* Some people use Uncle Sam as a savings bank. They will purposely allow Federal withholding tax on their incomes to be overdeducted by their employers, knowing that they will get a nice refund early the next year when they file their tax returns. This "forced saving" has the advantage of being taken from your paycheck before you can get at it, so, psychologically, you don't miss it. It is a substitute for the self-discipline necessary for other kinds of regular savings.

However, the disadvantage is that you are loaning the Government money, some of it for more than a year, *at no interest.* As an alternative, you could more precisely calculate your withholding tax burden and still use the "forced savings" approach by buying E bonds with the money through payroll savings, or have money deposited to your company credit union account, etc.

In fact, the way the tax rules read now, you must have at least 80% of your tax paid before the end of the year and 90% of the tax due at the end of any quarter paid in. This can be done by withholding or estimated tax payments or both. However, that still gives you the ability to "underwithhold" 10–20% of your tax due without penalty. If you underwithhold too much, there is a 7% per year penalty on the amount underwithheld that you'll have to pay to the Internal Revenue Service when they bill you.

The way you fine tune the withholding amount your employer deducts, is Form W-4, Employee Withholding Allowance Certificate. To adjust the amount withheld, you increase or decrease the number of exemptions that you claim. When you finally file your return by April 15, you must identify the exact exemptions to which you are entitled. Each exemption, under current tax regulations, reduces your taxable income by $750 per year. Depending on how often you are paid, the $750 is represented by the following amounts:

Payroll Period	Exemption amount/dependent
Weekly	$14.50
Semi-monthly	$31.30
Monthly	$62.50

If you have been accustomed to a refund of, say, $200 from IRS each spring, (the "loan" you made without interest) you can recapture the $200 from the clutches of IRS and put it in the credit union instead. Adding one exemption, via the W-4 form, produces about $240 less in withholding tax in a 32% tax bracket. Since the withholding amount does not have to be exact, you can invest the $240 over the year and use the interest you earn, about $7.44 at 6% in this example, to help build your retirement fund. It's not much, but every little bit helps these days.

A simple way to determine how much one exemption will save you in taxes withheld is to multiply $750 by your highest tax bracket, i.e., if 32%, then 32% of $750 equals $240. An easy-to-use table may help:

Tax Bracket %	Approximate value of one exemption
15%	$112.50
19%	$142.50
23%	$172.50
25%	$187.50
29%	$217.50
32%	$240.00
36%	$270.00
40%	$300.00
45%	$337.50
50%	$375.00
55%	$412.50
60%	$450.00
64%	$480.00
70%	$525.00

If you have been getting refunds of say, $500 from IRS and you are in the 25% bracket, use the W-4 to increase your exemptions by 3, reducing your withholding by $562.50. You'll have to pay back the $62.50 when you file your return, but in the meantime, you are earning interest on the $562.50 for up to a year or more.

None of these saving "tricks" are all that clever. They still require that you put up some money to get something, except for getting interest on demand deposits (#6) and taking advantage of billing cycles (#7). There are, however, some unexpected sources of money that do not require additional investment, but are available even if you haven't thought about them. We'll call these sources of "new" money.

C. Sources of "new" money

By "new" money is meant the capital that you can generate without additional investment on your part. These are sources of money that are not often considered as part of your income-producing assets. The following list of eight ideas will serve to illustrate the possibilities of "new" money.

1. UNUSED VACATION TIME

As you work longer for your employer, one of the benefits often inherent with length of service is vacation time. This is especially valuable if your employer allows you to save or defer vacation from year to year. This acts as a sort of savings account. For example, if you can save a vacation day from when you are earning, say $12,000 a year, until the day you retire, when you are earning $24,000, the effect is to double the value of that vacation day. Under this arrangement, when you retire, any unused vacation days would be paid off at your then achieved salary rate. Further, the vacation you are eligible to take this year was really earned last year. This year, you are earning vacation for next year. Therefore, if you retire this year, you will be paid off for any unused vacation earned last year, plus the vacation you earned for next year, plus any saved or deferred vacation. Let's take an example:

Date of hire—January 1
Date of retirement—June 30
Days deferred—8 weeks vacation (40 days)
Current annual vacation—5 weeks (25 days)

If you take no vacation in the year of retirement, you would accrue the following vacation allowance:

Earned from previous year—	25.0 days
Earned this year (6 months)—	12.5 days
Deferred vacation not taken—	40.0 days
Total—	77.5 days

Assuming an average of 22 working days per month, this would result in about 3½ months additional pay on retirement, or about 30% of your current salary. If you are earning at the rate of $24,000 per year, or $2000 per month, you would receive a "windfall" of $7000 to $7200 on retirement. You would have to pay income tax on this amount, of course, but since your total earnings for the year will probably be less than for the previous year, the tax will be relatively modest. In addition, if you retire late in the year—when you have collected most of your regular salary—the salary bump may enable you to use income tax Schedule G, Income Averaging, to further reduce your tax. Another possibility is to delay your retirement by a month or so in order to put the vacation pay into the next calendar and tax year. Investing this new-found money in an income-producing medium will give you additional retirement income, as well as an increase in assets.

Check your employer's benefit book to see how unused vacation works for your company, and plan your strategy consistent with the plan.

2. INCREASING RETURN ON INVESTMENT

Are you getting the standard passbook interest rate from your savings institution? If so, you're probably receiving about 5¼% for your money. Did you know that there are many places where you can get 6% or more in *insured* passbook savings? Did you know that all these places have bank-by-mail facilities and pay the postage both ways?

What does an increase of ¾ of 1% mean to you? Well, with daily compounding, at 5¼%, $1000 grows to $2222.97 in 15 years; at 6% it would grow to $2491.53. The difference, $268.56, is at no cost to you. The State of Maryland seems to have many of these savings and loan associations. To mention just a few:

Friendship Savings & Loan
5415 Friendship Blvd.
Chevy Chase, Md. 20015
(301) 654-4774

Chevy Chase Savings & Loan
8401 Connecticut Ave.
Chevy Chase, Md. 20015
(301) 652-1551

Laurel Building Association
201 N. Frederick Ave.
Gaithersburg, Md. 20760
(301) 948-2688

John Hanson Savings & Loan Inc.
7610 Penn Ave.
Forestville, Md. 20028
(301) 839-4600

Such associations offer passbook savings accounts which, under normal circumstances, pay withdrawals on demand. By tying your money up for longer periods of time, you can increase your return tremendously. These longer-term deposits are called "certificates of deposit" (CD's) or "savings certificates." As of this writing, CD's were paying 7¾% for 6-year certificates. Over the 15-year example we were using before, the $1000 (usually the minimum deposit), would grow to $3247.90, an increase of $1024.93 over the 5¼% passbook. That's over 46% more! However, don't put money you may need quickly into CD's. The penalties for early withdrawal are substantial, although in some cases it may be worthwhile to suffer the penalty if you must have the money for an unforseen emergency. *Tax Tip*: The penalties are tax deductible.

3. BUILDING ASSETS BY TAX SAVINGS

Current IRS taxes range from 15% to 70% on taxable income (See Table V in Chapter 4). If you could find a way to eliminate taxes on your income, you would be creating an additional source of "new" money, the money that would have been paid in taxes. It is this concept that makes certain investments attractive, even if the return does not appear very great on the surface.

The effect of federal income taxes

In fact, at this point, it may be worthwhile to review the effect of federal income taxes on interest rates. Table VI shows the real rate of return on an investment after federal taxes have been paid for various tax brackets. This real rate of return is reduced even more if the income is also taxed by state or local authorities. A 5¼% passbook interest rate, for example, in a 32% federal tax bracket, becomes a real interest rate of 3.57%; a 7¾% return becomes a 5.27% real return in the same tax bracket. Conversely, to get a real return of over 6% in a 32% federal tax bracket would require an investment returning nearly 9%! In Chapter 1, the advantage of IRA and Keogh retirement plans were discussed. These plans shelter capital from taxes by deferring payment of taxes on income. However, the day eventually comes when such income must be reported and the taxes paid.

TABLE VI. REAL INTEREST RATES ON TAXABLE INCOME.

Taxable Interest Rate	\multicolumn{7}{c}{Effective Rate after Taxes (in tax brackets indicated)}
	19%	25%	32%	36%	39%	45%	50%
5%	4.05%	3.75%	3.40%	3.20%	3.05%	2.75%	2.50%
5¼	4.25	3.94	3.57	3.36	3.20	2.89	2.62
5½	4.46	4.12	3.74	3.52	3.35	3.02	2.75
5¾	4.66	4.31	3.91	3.68	3.51	3.16	2.87
6%	4.86%	4.50%	4.08%	3.84%	3.66%	3.30%	3.00%
6¼	5.06	4.69	4.25	4.00	3.81	3.44	3.12
6½	5.26	4.87	4.42	4.16	3.96	3.57	3.25
6¾	5.47	5.06	4.59	4.32	4.12	3.71	3.37
7%	5.67%	5.25%	4.76%	4.48%	4.27%	3.85%	3.50%
7¼	5.87	5.44	4.93	4.64	4.42	3.99	3.62
7½	6.07	5.62	5.10	4.80	4.57	4.12	3.75
7¾	6.28	5.81	5.27	4.96	4.73	4.26	3.87
8%	6.48%	6.00%	5.44%	5.12%	4.88%	4.40%	4.00%
8¼	6.68	6.19	5.61	5.28	5.03	4.54	4.12
8½	6.88	6.38	5.78	5.44	5.18	4.67	4.25
8¾	7.09	6.56	5.95	5.60	5.34	4.81	4.37
9%	7.29%	6.75%	6.12%	5.76%	5.49%	4.95%	4.50%
9¼	7.49	6.94	6.29	5.92	5.64	5.09	4.62
9½	7.69	7.12	6.46	6.08	5.79	5.22	4.75
9¾	7.90	7.31	6.63	6.24	5.95	5.36	4.87
10%	8.10%	7.50%	6.80%	6.40%	6.10%	5.50%	5.00%
10¼	8.30	7.69	6.97	6.56	6.25	5.64	5.12
10½	8.50	7.87	7.14	6.72	6.40	5.77	5.25
10¾	8.71	8.06	7.31	6.88	6.56	5.91	5.37
11%	8.91%	8.25%	7.48%	7.04%	6.71%	6.05%	5.50%
11¼	9.11	8.44	7.65	7.20	6.86	6.19	5.62
11½	9.32	8.62	7.82	7.36	7.01	6.32	5.75
11¾	9.52	8.81	7.99	7.52	7.18	6.46	5.87
12%	9.72%	9.00%	8.16%	7.68%	7.32%	6.60%	6.00%

Taxes and real return on investments

There are ways to avoid income taxes completely. The whole arena of tax-exempt municipal bonds has this advantage. But, before we proceed further, let's consider the nature of a good investment. Any investment has at least three variables to be considered:

- Safety
- Liquidity
- Return (as a function of purchasing power)

In terms of safety, U.S. government obligations are considered the safest investment you can make, although every investment has an element of risk. Full faith and credit, backed by the taxing power of the federal government, stand behind these obligations. Similar safety up to the limits of the various plans for deposit insurance—currently at $40,000 per account—is extended to banks. Federally insured savings and loan associations, and so forth. Generally, *the higher the safety of an obligation, the lower the return*. Slightly below federal obligations in safety are municipal obligations backed by the full faith and credit of the jurisdiction. This would include state insured savings and loan associations. Somewhat below these in safety are revenue municipal bonds backed by the income specific to the obligation, such as bridge or highway tolls, rental income, water or sewage charges. And below these in safety come the various corporate obligations backed by a company's ability to maintain its profitability in a competitive marketplace. Therefore, the safest of financial obligations have some form of tax saving associated with them—federal, being exempt from state taxes, and municipals, being exempt from both federal taxes and taxes levied by the issuing states.

"Liquidity" refers to the ease with which you can get your money back when you want it. A checking account, passbook savings account, and money market fund are all highly liquid. A time related investment such as a bond or certificate of deposit is less liquid since you must hold the investment for some time or suffer a penalty or loss in value to cash it in before it's due. *Generally, the more liquid the obligation, the lower the return.*

"Return" is the reward you get for loaning money, or buying a piece of the company. When loaning money, the return is often fixed and related to time. When buying a share of the company, the return is keyed to the profitability of the company you are investing in, as well as the psychology of the marketplace. Return on loaned money, assuming the loanee doesn't go broke, will never be greater than the interest promised. Return on a share of stock may go terrifically high if the venture is a success, but the down-side risk of failure is much greater.

(One exception to the general differentiation of return for loaned money versus share investment is the convertible bond. This kind of security offers both the advantages and disadvantages of stocks and bonds. Basically, the convertible bond gives the holder the option of converting the bond into a specific number of common shares of stock, so the value of the bond is a function of the value of the underlying shares of common stock. You get a fixed return, yet have a chance to share in the growth of the company. For example, a convertible bond is issued for $5000 bearing a 5% coupon. It is also convertible into 100 shares of the issuing company which is selling for $50 per share at the time of issuance. Now, if the price of the stock rises to $60 per share, converting the bond to 100 shares would increase its value to $6000. On the other hand, if the common shares drop to $40 per share, there would be no advantage in converting and you would choose to continue to receive a return from the bond's fixed-income value at 5% per year. Because there are relatively few convertible bonds, the market for them is not as active as is the market for common stocks. As a result, convertible bonds may not be as liquid as other securities. The other difference is that, because of the convertibility option, the fixed rates of return on these issues may be slightly less than other competing fixed-return securities offered at the same time.)

Because the average layman just doesn't have the resources to evaluate these variables, rating services have cropped up which evaluate securities for you. They equate safety, liquidity, and return, and produce a scale for comparing one investment with another. An outline of the two major quality rating services and their rating systems follow.

Standard & Poor's	**Meaning**	**Moody's**
AAA	The best; no cause to worry	Aaa
AA	Excellent chance of repayment	Aa
A	Good chance of repayment	A
BBB	Slight risk of non-payment	Baa
BB	Some risk of non-payment	Ba
B	Speculative	B
CCC	Very speculative	C
NR	Not rated	NR

Generally, the higher the quality rating, the lower the return. Bonds in the first four categories are considered investment quality bonds. This does not mean that "B" rated bonds will not be paid off, but that the rating services believe the money history of the jurisdiction, the base on which the obligation will be funded, or the current extent of outstanding debt of the jurisdiction is such that it entails a greater risk than higher rated obligations. It is interesting to note, however, that even during the depths of the depression in the 1930s, more than 98% of the obligations of municipals were met without fail.

Looking at return as a function of purchasing power, then, if your after-tax real return is 5.27% and inflation is increasing prices of goods and services at 6%, it doesn't take a genius to see that you are falling .73% behind each year and that you can subsequently buy less with more money each year. Using our previous example of a 5¼% passbook savings resulting in a real return of 3.5%, you are falling 2.43% behind inflation after taxes. It is clear, therefore, that return, as it relates to purchasing power, will vary with tax brackets, interest rates, and rates of inflation. To keep ahead of inflation, you must generate a real return equal to or greater than the inflation rate.

Now, let's tie this discussion into our main concern at the moment—saving through the avoidance of taxes. Using the example of a person in the 32% federal tax bracket with a 6% taxable return on an investment of $1000, the taxpayer would have to deduct the tax from savings or other income—an amount of $19.20. If there were no taxes to pay, that tax money could be invested as another source of both assets and income. *Shifting assets from taxable-income-producing to non-taxable-income-producing accomplishes that end.* Table VII shows the return an investor would have to receive in order to match what would be retained from a non-taxable investment. If the interest of 6% is tax-free in the 32% tax bracket, the equivalent taxable investment would have to return 8.82% to generate the same net dollars. In this case, the non-taxable interest rate is the real interest rate and, if the investor had shifted, he would in effect be investing an additional $19.20 in the first year, $20.35 in the second, and so on.

To conclude, the source of "new" money in this case is the equivalent tax money saved, and these dollars can be projected as savings over time the same way any dollar savings can.

4. YOUR INSURANCE POLICIES

Some years ago you sat down with an insurance agent and you worked out an insurance program to cover your requirements while your family was growing up. Let's say it was for $50,000; if you died, your heirs would get a windfall, "free and clear." Right? No. Wrong!

TABLE VII. EQUIVALENT INTEREST RATES ON NON-TAXABLE INVESTMENTS.

Non-Taxable (Real) Interest Rate	\multicolumn{7}{c}{Equivalent rate needed if Taxable (in tax brackets indicated)}
	19%	25%	32%	36%	39%	45%	50%
3%	3.70%	4.00%	4.41%	4.69%	4.92%	5.45%	6.00%
3¼	4.01	4.33	4.78	5.08	5.33	5.91	6.50
3½	4.32	4.67	5.15	5.47	5.74	6.36	7.00
3¾	4.63	5.00	5.51	5.86	6.15	6.82	7.50
4%	4.94%	5.33%	5.88%	6.25%	6.56%	7.27%	8.00%
4¼	5.25	5.67	6.25	6.64	6.97	7.73	8.50
4½	5.56	6.00	6.62	7.03	7.38	8.18	9.00
4¾	5.86	6.33	6.99	7.42	7.79	8.64	9.50
5%	6.17%	6.67%	7.35%	7.81%	8.20%	9.09%	10.00%
5¼	6.48	7.00	7.72	8.20	8.61	9.55	10.50
5½	6.79	7.33	8.09	8.59	9.02	10.00	11.00
5¾	7.10	7.67	8.46	8.98	9.43	10.45	11.50
6%	7.41%	8.00%	8.82%	9.38%	9.84%	10.91%	12.00%
6¼	7.72	8.33	9.19	9.77	10.25	11.36	12.50
6½	8.02	8.67	9.56	10.16	10.66	11.82	13.00
6¾	8.33	9.00	9.93	10.55	11.07	12.27	13.50
7%	8.64%	9.33%	10.29%	10.94%	11.48%	12.73%	14.00%
7¼	8.95	9.67	10.66	11.33	11.88	13.18	14.50
7½	9.26	10.00	11.03	11.72	12.29	13.64	15.00
7¾	9.57	10.33	11.40	12.11	12.70	14.09	15.50
8%	9.88%	10.67%	11.76%	12.50%	13.11%	14.54%	16.00%
8¼	10.18	11.00	12.13	12.89	13.52	15.00	16.50
8½	10.49	11.33	12.50	13.28	13.93	15.45	17.00
8¾	10.80	11.67	12.87	13.67	14.34	15.91	17.50
9%	11.11%	12.00%	13.23%	14.06%	14.75%	16.36%	18.00%
9¼	11.42	12.33	13.60	14.45	15.16	16.82	18.50
9½	11.73	12.67	13.97	14.84	15.57	17.27	19.00
9¾	12.04	13.00	14.33	15.23	15.98	17.73	19.50
10%	12.35%	13.33%	14.70%	15.62%	16.39%	18.18%	20.00%

The real purpose of life insurance

Let's get down to basics. All those who know the real purpose of life insurance, raise your hands! Did you say, "To pay off the mortgage?" "Educate your children?" "Retire early?" If you did, you flunked the test. Life insurance has one real purpose—"protection"—to provide a dollar estate for your family if you don't live long enough to amass one for yourself.

The very fact that you are reading this book indicates that you have lived long enough to amass some estate already. How much of that $50,000 have you already earned? How much have you earned in your life insurance savings alone? Wait a minute! What is "savings" doing in there with "protection"? Well, if you bought any kind of policy other than term insurance, you have inadvertently invested in a savings account!

Insurance as a Savings Account?

How good a savings account has it been? Not so hot! Suppose when you were 25 years old you took out a $50,000 ordinary life policy and began paying a $650 annual premium to the insurance company. How would these investments compare, say, 22 years later at age 47, assuming you deposited this money in insured savings for an average of 4% annual interest?

Life Insurance

Total invested	$14,300	Cash surrender value of the policy — $12,293
Investment Value	$14,300 −12,293	Average *cost* per year = $91.22
Cost of insurance	$ 2,007	

Savings Account

Total deposited	$14,300	Value of account 22 years later — $21,772
Investment Value	$14,300 −21,772	Average *savings* per year = $339.63
Increase in savings	$ 7,472	

"Now, wait a minute," you say, "you didn't include the cost of insurance during those years." Fair enough, let's assume today's rates for a five-year renewable term policy:

Age	Annual Premium on $50,000	Number of Years	Total Paid	Difference Over Savings Account	
25–29	$172.40	5	$ 862	Savings increase	$7472
30–34	190.04	5	950	Cost of term	−5192
35–39	225.32	5	1127	Net savings	
40–44	290.00	5	1450	benefit	$2280
45–49	401.72	2	803		
50–54	584.00	0	—		
55–59	866.24	0	—		
			$5192		

Still an advantage for the savings account! How is this possible? Read your insurance policy. You are probably getting 2½% or 2¾% interest in your policy. Even assuming a modest 4% savings account interest over that same period, you would do better in savings. In addition, about 15% of your premium payments go to commissions for insurance agents. There are, of course, no such charges for savings accounts.

Another point: What is the insurance company really insuring you for? "$50,000," you say. Sorry, wrong again. They are insuring you for $50,000 *less the cash surrender value of the policy*; so in our example, at age 47, you really have only $37,707 worth of insurance and $12,293 of cash surrender value; when the policy matures (that is, when you die), the insurance company keeps the cash surrender value when paying your heirs the $50,000. If you cashed the policy in, investing the cash and bought *term insurance* for the difference, you could have your capital without having to die for it, and still maintain the needed protection! For example, $37,707 in term insurance at age 47 would cost about $8.034 per every $1000 of insurance, or $302.94 versus $650 for a $50,000 ordinary life policy. That's a savings of $347.06. In addition, interest on $12,293 at 6% would be $737.58. So instead of a $50,000 program costing you $650, it would profit you $434.64, a swing of nearly $1085. The next year you'd need only $36,622 of term insurance, reducing more and more each year.

You ask, "Isn't that drastic, cashing my life policy in? Why not just borrow the cash surrender value?" Good thought, but the fact is that your policy will probably require an interest payment of 5% to 6% due on the amount borrowed, while you are only getting 2½% to 2¾% from the insurance company. That is hardly a fair deal. (In spite of the bad deal, you can still make 1% or 2% on your cash surrender value if

Borrowing against life insurance?

outside interest rates remain above the insurance borrowing rates.) The only really valid reason you should not cash in your life policy is if your health might affect your ability to acquire needed term insurance. Even so, you can always acquire your new term insurance before cancelling your ordinary life insurance.

Converting life insurance to term insurance and savings

Let's look at the procedure again to see where the savings occur:

Term insurance program at the outset	Converting to a term insurance program later
• Buy term insurance for amount desired.	• Cash in policy, buying difference between it and amount desired in term insurance.
• Invest or save the difference in program cost between term and other life insurance.	• Invest cash, which will increase in value, enabling you to reduce amount of term insurance needed each year.
• Requires a discipline to save the difference regularly. If you can save your own money, you can keep what the insurance companies now take from you.	• Invest differences in premiums between reduced amount of term needed and former non-term policy, further reducing term insurance needed.
• Reduce amount of term insurance as cash savings build up.	

With this plan of approach, your insurance becomes a "living legacy" which you'll finally have in hand before you die. You'll be able to convert it to an income-producing asset while you're still alive, and also have the protection it represents. A calculation comparing conversion to *5-year renewable term, decreasing term,* or *paid-up insurance and term* shows the ranking of investment values in Table VIII.

The technique you use for conversion marginally favors decreasing term insurance until age 72, at which point 5-year renewable term would have been a better choice. In the case of 5-year renewable term, the total available for investment is more than the coverage desired at age 64, at which point the income on the $50,000 could be used to augment retirement. This happens at age 66 for converting to paid-up insurance and term, although it can be seen that this approach is least effective of the three in dollars produced. It happens at age 64 for the decreasing term plan, when the savings exceed coverage requirements and allow term insurance to be held to a later age.

TABLE VIII. COMPARISON OF 3 PLANS OF TERM INSURANCE.

Age	Investment Percentage of Term	5 year Renew. Term	Decreasing Term	Paid-Up & Term
47	30–45% term	3	1	2
48	30–45% term	3	1	2
49	30–45% term	2	3	1
50	30–45% term	1	3	2
51	30–45% term	1	3	2
52	25–36% term	2	1	3
53	25–36% term	2	1	3
54	25–36% term	2	1	3
55	25–36% term	2	1	3
56	25–36% term	1	2	3
57	18–27% term	3	1	2
58	18–27% term	2	1	3
59	18–27% term	2	1	3
60	18–27% term	2	1	3
61	18–27% term	2	1	3
62	6–20% term	3	1	2
63	6–20% term	2	1	3
64	6–20% term	2	1	3
65	6–20% term	2	1	3
66	0–16% term	2	1	3
67	0–7½% term	2	1	3
68	0–7½% term	2	1	3
69	0–7½% term	2	1	3
70	0–7½% term	2	1	3
71	0–7½% term	2	1	3
72	All savings	1	2	3
73	All savings	1	2	3

Total Value of Coverage Ranking

In short, you can have your cake and eat it, too. You can receive your insurance program in cash, before you die, making you happy and your family, too. Further, instead of a fixed lump of money, after it reaches the amount you need for the program, the income it produces can be added to your retirement income—if $50,000, an extra $3000 or more per year—and the $50,000 asset still remains part of your estate.

In conclusion, you don't make your auto insurance company a savings bank, nor your homeowner's insurance company, nor your health insurance company. Why should you try to do it with life insurance? Convincing you that their life insurance policies are a sound proposition is the way insurance agents earn that 15% fee. Resist the temptation and earn retirement money instead.

Receiving your benefits before you die

5. DISCOUNT BONDS

The nature of bonds: real growth vehicles

Up to this point, we have been looking at investments on a 100% basis—that is, the direct return on investment calculated by multiplying the face value times a given rate of interest. For example, a $5000 investment at 6% interest will return $300 simple interest, or $307 compounded quarterly, $308.50 compounded monthly, or $313.75 if compounded daily. (See Table A in the Appendix.)

Many money instruments, such as bonds, are traded in a secondary market. The face value of a bond—say, $5000—will always remain the same, as will the face interest rate, also called the coupon interest rate. When this bond matures, you will be paid $5000 for the bond, regardless of the price you actually paid for it. The price you actually pay for the bond is a function of market psychology, the going rate of interest in the outside money market, the faith of the investing public in the jurisdiction or institution, and the bond's rating. In short, you may pay more than $5000 for a bond with a high interest rate, or less than $5000 for a bond with a low rate. The real rate received on the money invested will approximate the interest rates prevailing in the current money market, all else being equal.

Calculating the return on discount bonds

You can use this phenomenon to your advantage by making your bond portfolio, in your capital-growth investment stage, reflect the growth potential of bonds. If a $5000 bond sold originally with a 3½% coupon rate, every six months that bond will pay $87.50 until it matures, or $175 per year. Now suppose interest rates have risen since the bond was issued, so that the bond can now be purchased in the open market for $3000. The bond still pays $175 per year, so your return on investment is over 5.83%. Not too bad! But the really exciting thing is that, if you hold the bond to maturity, you will receive $5000 from the issuer of the bond, a guaranteed capital gain of $2000 on a $3000 investment.

Granted, you have to pay capital gains tax on the gain of $2000, but if you plan the maturity dates properly, that money gain may not occur until after you retire, reducing the tax liability even more. Let's take an example of how to figure return on investment on a discounted bond:

Given

Face Value—$5000—Matures in 16 years
Coupon interest rate—3½%
Interest Dollars—$175 per year
Price you pay for the bond—$3000
Your income tax bracket is 28%

Calculate

A. Return on face value: $175/5000 = 3½%
B. Return on investment: $175/3000 = 5.83%
C. Return to maturity:
   1. $2000 gain/16 years = $125 per year
   2. Tax: $2000/2 × 28% tax rate = $280/16 years = $17.50 per year
   3. $175 + $125 − $17.50 = $282.50 per year
   4. $282.50/3000 = 9.416%

A return of 9.416% is growth by anyone's definition! Further, if this was a municipal bond, the after-tax return, or real return to you, would be 9.416%. To get the equivalent taxable return in the 28% tax bracket would require about a 13% return on your money.

So, for a given investment situation, discount bonds provide a technique for increasing capital as well as receiving an acceptable return on investment. Most bonds pay interest semi-annually and bonds are issued every month of the year. A bond portfolio of six bonds, if properly selected, could provide a monthly income.

You may ask how a $5000 bond is available for $3000. Often, the original purchaser may need the cash, or may want to establish a tax loss, or decide to swap bonds to both establish a tax loss and still keep equivalent bonds. In any case, your stockbroker will be delighted to look into the discount bond market for you.

How bond prices are quoted

Bond prices are often quoted as a percentage of face value. A bond selling at "100" would sell for 100% of face value; "60" at 60% of face value (a discount bond); or "115" at 115% of face value (a "premium" bond). Premium bonds usually have extraordinarily high yields or are extremely safe investments. When the bond matures, however, the amount over 100% you paid the bond seller is not paid back to you and, unfortunately, cannot be considered as a capital loss for tax purposes.

Callable bonds

A thing to watch for in bonds is a "call date." This is the date that the bond can be redeemed by the issuer, before normal maturity. A bond may be issued for 25 years but "callable" in 10 years. This is a device the bond issuer uses to hedge against interest rates. If interest rates drop after the bond is issued, and the jurisdiction or organization can refinance the loan at a lower rate, they can retire the outstanding bonds by "calling" them early. A modest premium is sometimes paid for the call privilege by the bond issuer. Interestingly, bonds with lower interest rates are less likely to be called since the current rates are generally higher. When you buy a discount bond, you have two other things going for you: (1) the bond is less likely to be called, giving you an uninterrupted investment over a longer time; and (2) if called, you will collect the face value and resulting capital gain sooner, which may not be all bad.

Commissions on bonds

Another point on bonds: The commission charged is much less than the cost of an equivalent dollar trade in stocks, and it is often buried in the price of the bond itself rather than tacked on as a separate charge. Also, you do not lose any interest on buying or selling bonds since the interest is calculated in the price as of the day of trade.

Insurance for municipal bonds

Although municipal bonds are not insured, it is possible, now, to protect your investment in them. Several companies are offering to review municipal bond portfolios, and if the risks are reasonable, they will agree to insure them for prompt payment of interest when due and for payment of principal when the bond matures.

Some typical holdings might cost an average of about .2% (1/5 of 1%) of the face value of the portfolio per year to insure. A $50,000 face value portfolio would cost about $100 per year to protect. The bonds do not necessarily have to be highly rated or rated at all, but, clearly, the lower the rating or higher the risk, the higher the insurance premium.

Not all states permit this sort of insurance to be written. As of mid-1977, insurance was not available in Kansas, Minnesota, New Jersey, and Texas.

Considering the high likelihood that municipal jurisdictions will repay their debts, you will have to judge for yourself whether the payment of the insurance premium is worth the cost. Further, most companies set a minimum amount of portfolio face value before they will insure bonds. Often, this is $50,000 or more, so if your holdings are modest, you may not be eligible for such insurance.

6. "LIQUIFYING" YOUR HOME

In Chapter 3, some discussion was made of non-income-producing assets and their cost as it relates to reducing current income. The point was that non-income-producing assets would have to be made liquid before they could be converted to income-producing assets. In many cases this would mean disposing of the asset for cash, which could then be invested. Stamps, gold bars, coin collections, vehicles, furs, jewelry, furniture, and so forth, are all assets in this category. However, there is one non-income-producing asset that may be profitably "converted" without disposing of the asset. It is one, however, that must be examined carefully before taking the plunge, since it's your home!

Assuming that the equity in your home is greater than the outstanding mortgage on the home, you have a dollar asset source which is idly "sitting there." For example, if your home is appraised or selling in the open market for $80,000, and your present mortgage balance is $20,000, your equity is $60,000, which is not drawing any return. Whether it pays to "liquify" this equity is a function of several variables:

- Outside investment rates of return
- The cost of money
- The length of the loan period
- Your federal income tax bracket
- Tax regulations
- The amount of "guts" you have, since you would be substantially increasing your outstanding debt

A house can be "liquified" in at least two ways. One is to get a second trust or second mortgage on your home. This technique is limited by lending institutions to only part of the equity in the house, and it involves a very high rate of interest. In early 1977, 10½% to 12% was the typical range of interest rates required for a second trust over a 10-year period. If, however, you were in the 50% federal tax bracket, the real cost of interest after taxes would be 5¼% to 6%, the 36% bracket, 6.75% to 7.68%, and so forth. (See Table VI, Real Interest Rates on Taxable Income). If you can find an investment that will provide a guaranteed return greater than the real cost of interest, you may be dollars ahead—for example, as mentioned in the previous section, a discount bond. Let's look at the arithmetic to illustrate the principle:

Second mortgage trusts and second mortgages: Do they pay?

Given

Mortgage loan—$8,000, 10 Years.

Rate—10½% simple interest per year

Calculate

Interest cost	$840.00 × 10 yrs =	$8400
Less tax savings (39% bracket)	−327.60 × 10 yrs =	−3276
	$512.40 × 10 yrs =	$5124

Given

Discount $10,000 bond—$8,000
Matures in 10 years

Rate—6% simple interest per year

Calculate

Return on face	$600 × 10 yrs =	$6000
Return to maturity		
1. $2000/10 yrs	+200 × 10 yrs =	2000
2. Capital gain tax	−39 × 10 yrs =	−390
3. Tax on interest (39%)	−234 × 10 yrs =	−2340
	$527 × 10 yrs =	$5270

Real return $527.00 × 10 yrs = $ 5270
Less real loan cost −512.40 × 10 yrs = −5124
$ 14.60 × 10 yrs = $ 146

Real cost % = $512.40/$8000 = 6.41%
Real rate of return = $527/8000 = 6.59%

At the end of the 10-year period, your loan would be due, but your bond would also mature, enabling you to pay off the loan and keep your profit. The bulk of the profit from the whole transaction occurs when you receive payment for the matured bond. However, the purpose of this exercise is only to illustrate a principle that may be used to your advantage. It is not intended as a recommendation.

Refinancing your home: a modest income opportunity

The second approach to "liquifying" your home is by refinancing. This means paying off your existing mortgage and assuming a new first mortgage on your home. In our example, the $20,000 existing mortgage would be paid off and a new loan of up to, say, $60,000, would be taken out, leaving you $40,000 for investment. The calculation of this relationship is quite complicated since the typical mortgage includes payment on principal as well as interest in the monthly payment. Again, the purpose of this section is to illustrate a principle, not to make a recommendation. The three advantages of refinancing over the second mortgage are:
- A larger amount of equity can be borrowed, often 75%
- First mortgage rates are often lower, about 8½% to 9% in early 1977
- The term of the loan is usually longer, often 20 to 30 years

Recognizing the inadequacy of comparison, we will not attempt a mathematic proof, but rather state that the return you may receive on this form of financing may net you less than 1% on investment. In order to determine whether "liquifying" is worth the effort, other costs must be considered in your final calculation, including pre-payment penalties, appraisal costs, and "floating" mortgage rates. You'll need the help of an expert on mortgage financing to determine the viability of this whole approach.

In addition, the tax consequences of such a transaction must be carefully examined since you may not be able to deduct interest costs from income under certain conditions—if you buy tax-free securities, for example. Again, you will need a tax expert to help determine your tax liability. The refinancing approach involves a multi-step investment:
- Tax savings on mortgage interest
- Buying taxable securities
- Converting the net return from taxable securities to non-taxable ones, such as a municipal bond fund

A general conclusion. You really have to be hard pressed for additional income to go through the trouble of refinancing a house at today's high interest rates. Unfortunately, even if interest rates came down on mortgages, it's likely that interest rates on the securities you want to buy would have come down also. If this approach to producing income is to have any merit, the key is the spread between these interest rates. But get expert help before you leap; and even then, think twice.

Because of the incredible growth in housing prices, some new approaches to mortgage financing are being explored by lenders. Many of these ideas are intended to help the building industry sell to a potential buyer even if the buyer's current purchasing power is low. Some of these approaches are:

- Graduated mortgage payments—payments start low, then rise with the buyer's income.
- Variable rate mortgages—rates float up or down with the money markets.
- Interest-only loans—buyer would pay only interest for a specified time, followed by a "balloon" payment of principal.
- Sharing the value—buyer shares increased equity in the home with the lender or builder in exchange for a lower downpayment and lower interest rates.

Some of these ideas have real applicability to the retirement situation. For example:

- Reverse-annuity mortgage—enables people who have paid off their mortgage to remain in their home, yet add to income from the house equity. The lender pays the borrower a fixed monthly sum based on a percentage of the current value of the property. The loan comes due when the borrower dies and is paid off through probate.
- Line-of-credit mortgage—enables the buyer to borrow against the increasing equity in the home to meet major family expenses at fairly low rates. The borrower could use the loan to pay for a college education, make home improvements, and so forth.

Pressure for change is presently on Congress for legislation to validate these experiments.

7. SOME NEW APPROACHES TO MORTGAGE FINANCING

There is nothing magical about the age of 65, but some interesting financial things happen then. Consider:

- Additional exemption of $750 for age on your tax return
- Possible qualification for Credit for the Elderly using Schedules R and RP on the income tax forms

8. THE "SENIOR CITIZEN" ADVANTAGE

73

- Reduced prices for movies, haircuts, hairdresser, etc.
- Eligibility for Medicare
- A colossal savings on the gain realized from the sale of your residence

Since the first four are obvious or modest in value, we needn't discuss them further; but the last can prove an important source of "new" money. If you sell or exchange your residence and:

1. were 65 years of age or older before selling, and
2. owned and used the property as your principal residence for a time period totaling at least five of the last eight years before the sale, and
3. have never used this exclusion before (it's a once in a lifetime shot), then you may exclude the *entire* gain from capital gains taxes if the adjusted sales price is $35,000 or less. If more than $35,000, then a portion of the gain is eligible for exclusion. If the property is jointly owned, when either owner is over 65, the rules still apply.

The first thing to do is determine the "adjusted sales price." Let's consider two examples:

	Example I	Example II
Selling price of residence	$80,000	$39,400
Less: Commissions and expenses of sale (advertising, legal fees, etc.)	−5,500	−2,900
Equals: Amount realized	$74,500	$36,500
Less: Fixing-up expenses (painting and repairs within 90 days of sale)	−1,500	−1,500
Equals: Adjusted sales price	$73,000	$35,000

Next, compute the "exclusion factor." If the adjusted sales price is $35,000 or less, do not report the gain. If it is over $35,000:

	Example I	Example II
Divide: Adjusted sales price into $35,000	35000/73000	35000/35000
Equals: Exclusion factor	.479452	1.0

Then, the "Gain on the Sale":

	Example I	Example II
Amount realized	$74,500	$36,500
Less: Basis of residence sold (original cost plus improvements)	−44,000	−10,000
Equals: Gain on the sale	$30,500	$26,500

Finally, calculate the "exclusion" and Taxable Gain:

Gain on the sale	$30,500	$26,500
Times: the exclusion factor	× .479452	× 1.0
Equals: excludable portion of gain	$14,623.29	$26,500
Gain on the sale	$30,500.00	$26,500
Less: excludable portion of gain	−14,623.29	−26,500
Equals: Taxable gain	$15,876.71	$ 0

The taxable gain is reported as income using Schedule D of the tax forms (as a long term capital gain). Under present rules, taxes would be paid on 50% of the gain, or on $7938.36 in Example I. Even if the seller were in the 50% tax bracket, the actual tax paid would be $3969.18 on a profit of $30,500. So, the sale results in receipt of a net of $73,000 less taxes, say $3000, leaving $70,000 as investment for retirement income.

In Example II, which shows costs typical of houses bought 30–40 years ago, the gain of $26,500 is free and clear. Consider if the houses in question were sold one day *before* the 65th birthday. Again assuming a 50% tax bracket, Example I would require payment of tax on ½ of $30,500, and Example II on ½ of $26,500. That one day would cost $3655.82 (that is, $7625-$3939.18) in Example I, and $6625 in Example II.

If you have a choice, *choose to wait until after age 65 to sell your house and earn money for retirement.*

D. Filling Out the Sources of "New" Money form

All this "stashing away" business is intended to increase income-producing assets after retirement in order to augment retirement income. Using the new-found knowledge from this section, you are now prepared to fill our Exhibit V, the Sources of "New" Money form. A sample of this form appears at the end of this chapter, and a blank form for your own use can be found at the back of the book.

1. Follow along on Exhibit V while we enter examples of our "savings tricks." By pretending that FICA deductions continue all year, approximately $100 every two weeks for 7 months will be saved each year, or $1400. This plan will be used for 9 years until retirement. With 6% interest, it will grow to $14,686 in the retirement year. (Example from Appendix Table C: 8 years interest at 6% = 10.49 x $1400 = $14,686.)

2. Your spouse works and is not covered by a pension plan. You set up an IRA using 15% of her gross earnings and save a total of about

$1000 per year. Part of the earnings are sheltered as well as the interest. This will grow to $10,490 by retirement year. (Same formula as in #1 above.)

3. Using the ideas of "saving trick" #6, a $2000 checking/savings account will result in interest of $100 per year for 8 years, plus 5% interest compounded; $1049 is saved by the retirement year.

4. By shifting income-producing assets of $5000 from taxable to non-taxable situation, the $300 in interest becomes tax exempt. This results in tax savings of $300 x 40% tax bracket, or $120 per year for 8 years compounded. This grows to $1258 by retirement.

EXHIBIT V. **SOURCES OF "NEW" MONEY (Sample).**

		Year: Age:	1976 47	1983 54	1984 55	1996 67
	1. Savings—continue FICA from salary: $100 per pay period for 7 months (9 years)		1,400	12,460	14,686	14,686
(XT)	2. Spouse Earnings and IRA— $1000 per year for 8 years		1,000	8,900	10,490	10,490
	3. Interest on checking account— $2000 × 5% = $100 per year for 8 years		100	890	1,049	1,049
(XT)	4. Tax savings—shift to tax-free: $300 × 40% tax bracket for 8 years		120	1,068	1,258	1,258
	5. Increase return on investment—$7000 × ¾% for 8 years		52	462	545	545
	6. Company 25-year service gift— $1000 for 4 years (rec'd in 1980)		—	1,190	1,260	1,260
	7. Deferred vacation payment— 65 + days		—	—	10,000	10,000
	8. Convert insurance program to term and invest balance		—	—	—	32,000
	Total "new" money		2,672	24,970	39,288	71,288

5. Increased return on an investment of $7000 is accomplished by moving $2000 in miscellaneous assets to a 6% passbook, and by moving $5000 in savings and loan funds from a 6% passbook to a 2-year, 6¾% certificate of deposit. Increase is ¾% for 8 years, resulting in an additional $545 in retirement assets.

6. The employee's company pays $1000 after 25 years of service with the company. This money will grow to $1260 at 6% in 4 years. (Example from Table B: 6% for 4 years = 1.26 x $1000 = $1260.)

7. From unused and deferred vacation, the employee will be paid off for 65+ days of vacation, or 3 months pay. At $40,000 salary, 3/12, or 25% of this represents $10,000 in the retirement year.

8. The person has a permanent insurance program of $32,000. Using the approaches described in this chapter, by converting to a combination of term insurance and investment of the cash surrender value, by age 64, the entire program can be converted to cash worth $32,000. In that year, the income from the cash can be used to augment retirement income.

These assets should be totaled and posted to the Retirement Plan, and income from the assets should be posted to the income portion of the plan. Exhibit II has been expanded, and in Chapter 6, you'll use this information to "smooth out" the retirement plan, Exhibit VI.

6. Smoothing out the retirement plan

Effect of "new" money on short-fall

The "smoothed out" Retirement Plan at the end of this chapter, Exhibit VI, is the same as Exhibit II in Chapter 3, with the addition of the assets calculated for the Sources of "New" Money form in Chapter 5, and of the retirement income resulting from these assets. Let's assume that the new assets earn 6% of asset value as income. Reflecting also those investments that are tax-exempt, it can be seen, comparing Exhibit II and Exhibit VI, that in the first full year after retirement another $2357 in "new" money (from $39,288 in new assets) is attained. Of course, this takes care of the short-fall observed in Chapter 4 and on Exhibit I, the Expense Approximater. In fact, by comparing equivalent years, it can be seen that the short-fall of 1985 is not only wiped away, but substantial surpluses should be left each year for either augmenting your expense budget, or for additional savings in order to increase income even more. Here's what the projection looks like:

	1976	1985	1994	1998
Total expenses (from Exhibit I)	$43,220	$23,682	$19,766	$19,709
Annual income—first cut (from Exhibit II)	43,220	23,494	29,755	32,049
First long- or short-fall	$ 0	−$ 188	+$ 9,989	+$12,340
Annual income—smoothed out (from Exhibit VI)	$43,380	$25,851	$32,112	$36,326
Smoothed long- or short-fall	+$ 160	+$ 2,169	+$12,346	+$16,617

Some interesting observations can be made:
1. *Income grows.* Total income gradually grows from early retirement and improves by over 40% until it becomes fixed.
2. *Return on investment improves.* Return on investment, mentioned in Chapter 2 as 4.2% on invested asset value today, really has improved as a result of higher returns,

Year	1976	1983	1984	1985	1992	1996
Total Assets	$162,593	$262,851	$289,744	$289,744	$289,744	$321,744
Non-Salary Income	6,880	12,428	18,197	25,851	32,112	36,326
Return on Assets	4.23%	4.73%	6.28%	8.92%	11.08%	11.29%

greater tax exemption, and the start of Social Security (which is not income produced from personal assets). Observe this phenomenon from our smoothed-out Retirement Plan (Exhibit VI):

3. *Amount of taxable income decreases.* The amount of income taxable under federal income tax laws drops dramatically over the years. This is because you're gradually transferring your investment portfolio to tax-exempt situations, because of tax-exempt Social Security payments, and because after age 65 you and your spouse can claim increased personal exemptions. Naturally, if the taxable income decreases, and the tax rates remain unchanged, tax liability will go down, thus increasing spendable income for the retiree.

4. *Estate taxes are minimal.* Under the new estate tax procedures, the final assets of $321,744, plus whatever non-income-producing assets must be added to that sum, are subject to a marital exemption of one half the estate or $250,000 (whichever is greater) before the taxable estate is calculated, as shown in the Appendix Table D. Will assets of $321,744 be subject to estate taxes? Let's make some assumptions:

$321,744	Income producing assets
80,000	Family home
25,000	Silverware, collections, jewelry, etc.
5,000	Vehicles
10,000	Miscellaneous
$441,744	
−250,000	Marital deduction
$191,744	
−175,625	Equivalent estate tax credit (1981 and beyond)
$16,119	Taxable estate
× .32	Assumed estate tax rate of 32%
$5,158.08	Amount of estate tax

"FLOWER BONDS"   Does that mean your heirs will have to pay $5,158.08 out of the estate in taxes? Not necessarily. Suppose there are a few classes of U.S. Treasury bonds selling at discount, with a special advantage built into the bargain. You buy them at discount, but the U.S. Treasury will redeem them at par, prior to maturity, if used to pay federal estate taxes—up to the amount equalling the federal estate tax due! These bonds are euphemistically called "flower bonds," since the savings in estate taxes are said to be enough to pay for flowers at the funeral.

However, flower bonds are fast vanishing since the last one was offered by the U.S. Treasury in March, 1971. The last such bond available therefore matures in 1992. The interest coupons on the bonds range from 3-4¼%, but they sell for a discount price of about $750 for a bond of $1000 face amount. The Tax Reform Act of 1976 doesn't distinguish between flowers and other securities, as previous tax regulations did. Consequently, the capital gain on flowers is now taxable to the estate. In fact, if the flowers were not held 9 months in 1977 and 12 months starting in 1978, the gain would be short-term. Therefore, as a death-bed investment, flower bonds are somewhat less attractive than they used to be; but they can still serve to reduce the shrinkage of your estate by taxes. The basic problem is that, with the longer periods they must be held in order to qualify for long-term capital gain, return on investment will be limited to the low coupon rates on the bonds.

Incidentally, any state inheritance taxes paid are credited against any Federal estate taxes dues.

EXHIBIT VI. RETIREMENT PLAN (Sample) — SMOOTHED OUT.

		Now	Last Full Yr. Before Retirement	Target Retirement Year	1st Full Year After Retirement	Husband Soc. Sec.; Full	Fixed Income; Wife Soc. Sec.
INCOME	Year:	1976	1983	1984	1985	1992	1996
	Age:	47	54	55	56	63	67
Salary & Commissions		36500	40000	23333	0	0	0
Municipal Bonds - 6.1%		2257xt	2372xt	2372xt	2372xt	2635xt	2745xt
Muni. Bond Fund - 6%		0	1420ft	1649ft	1649ft	1649ft	1649ft
Company Stock - $7 Dividend		1330	1820	1890	1414	0	0
No. 1 Sav. & Loan Co. - 8%		800	1303	1326	1326	1326	1326
No. 2 Sav. & Loan Co. - 6%		1014	1610	1712	1712	1712	1712
Spouse Savings - 6¼%		942	1599	1687	1687	1687	1687
E Bonds - 6%		0	0	Conv. to H Bonds	1031st	1031st	1031st
Mutual Fund Dividend - 7%		377	644	690	690	690	690
Misc. Assets - 5¼%		0	162	162	162	162	162
Savings From Stock Sale - 6%		0	0	0	1006ft	4050ft	4050ft
*Personal Resources Income		43220	50930	34821	13049	14942	15052
Company Retirement		0	0	4352	10445	10445	10445
Social Security		0	0	0	0	4368xt	6552xt
**New Money		160	1498	2357	2357	2357	4277
*Total Income		43380	52428	41530	25851	32112	36326
*Taxable Income (Fed.)		41056	48038	36804	20119	18705	20625
Taxable Capital Gains		0	0	0	3400	0	0
ASSETS — INCOME-PRODUCING							
Municipal Bonds - 6.1%		50000	50000	50000	50000	50000	50000
Muni. Bond Fund - 6%		2257	23675	27490	27490	27490	27490
Company Stock		47500	65000	67500	50625	0	0
No. 1 Sav. & Loan Co. - 8%		10000	18392	19744	19744	19744	19744
No. 2 Sav. & Loan Co. - 6%		16900	26871	28561	28561	28561	28561
Spouse Savings - 6¼%		15700	25591	27004	27004	27004	27004
E Bonds - 6%		10177	16181	17199	17199	17199	17199
Mutual Fund - 7%		5387	9211	9858	9858	9858	9858
Misc. Assets - 5¼%		2000	2960	3100	3100	3100	3100
Savings From Stock Sale - 6%		0	0	0	16875	67500	67500
*Assets		159921	237881	250456	250456	250456	250456
**New Money		2672	24970	39288	39288	39288	71288
*Total Assets		162593	262851	289744	289744	289744	321744

7. Developing a financial plan of action

By this time, you should have a pretty fair idea of whether you will be able to retire, when, and with how much in resources. What's needed now is an organized plan to implement those steps necessary to effect your financially secure retirement.

Too little planning—a widespread problem

A survey in late 1976 revealed some appalling things about executives earning over $50,000—very few have done much in the way of personal financial planning. It can be assumed that the situation is even worse for people earning less. Some of the findings include:

- In only 80% of the cases did both husband and wife have a last will and testament. In many of these cases the will had not been updated to reflect a geographic change of residence.
- Fewer than 5% had an "umbrella" liability policy covering up to $1,000,000 in risks excluded from other policies. Supplemental insurance of this nature costs less than $100 per year.
- 75% did not have a systematic savings plan.
- Fewer than 33% had any real idea of how they would finance their retirement.
- Fewer than 5% had set up some plan to finance the cost of college for their children through trusts or gifts that enable the income to be taxed, if at all, at the youngster's tax rates.
- 90% were overconcentrated in their own company stock, resulting in an unbalanced portfolio. Most maintained such a portfolio because of simple inertia—lack of time or interest to improve their investment position.

The fundamental flaw in these people's personal finances was lack of a coherent plan.

Now, this kind of advice is available from investment and financial counselors for $4000–5000 per head. You can do virtually the same thing with the lessons learned in this book, and for the price of this book (which, incidentally, is probably tax deductible as "tax advice" under miscellaneous Deductions on your income tax form).

What is a Plan of Action?

A plan of action is a dated, sequenced checklist of things you must do to put your financial house in order. At the end of this chapter, you'll find a simple Financial Plan of Action (Exhibit VII). The exact order or timing of your own financial moves will depend on (1) how effectively you have planned up to now, (2) your resources, and (3) your willingness to overcome "financial inertia." Of these, the third is probably most crucial—stop stalling, plan your actions, and do it!

For your convenience a Checklist of Planning Actions is provided (Table IX). Use this Checklist to complete your own Plan of Action. Note that no blank form for your own Plan has been included in the Appendix. All you need this time is a pad of paper and plenty of thought.

One last point on Plans: they may change over time. This whole exercise is only valuable if it is maintained up to date. Company retirement or Social Security benefits may change and interest rates will go up and down (you will have to be alert to capitalize on upswings—a good rule to remember is to lock in the highest rate you can get for as long as you can get it). In fact you should review and update your Retirement Plan, at least on an annual basis. This will pin-point areas of opportunity and changes you should make to improve your retirement prospects.

TABLE IX. **CHECKLIST OF PLANNING ACTIONS.**

I Have Done This	I Have Not Done This	I Plan To Do This By: (Date)	
			Social Security • Requested an annual "Statement of Wages" from Social Security? • Filed for Social Security numbers for my children? • Gotten the latest retirement information from my local Social Security Office? *Company Retirement Plan* • Reviewed policy on payment of earned and deferred vacation upon retirement? • Reviewed benefits projected under company retirement plan? • Reviewed "joint and survivor" benefits under company retirement plan? • Can I contribute to plan to increase benefits?

continued on following page

CHECKLIST OF PLANNING ACTIONS (continued).

I Have Done This	I Have Not Done This	I Plan To Do This By: (Date)	

Own Retirement Plans
- Am I eligible for an IRA or Keogh retirement plan?
- Is my spouse eligible for an IRA or Keogh retirement plan?
- Have I investigated annuities?
- Do both my spouse and I have current wills?

Resources and Savings
- Do I have a systematic plan for savings?
- Have I shopped for the highest rate of return on insured savings?
- Have I explored municipal bond funds?
- Can I arrange to get interest on my checking account?
- Are certificates of deposit for me?
- Can I increase capital with discount municipal bonds?
- Are there non-income-producing assets that I can liquify or convert for income?
- Should I convert my E bonds to H bonds for income?
- Is my stock portfolio doing what I want it to do—increase in value or produce income?

Insurance Program
- Am I adequately protected in case of liability with an "umbrella" policy?
- Can I profitably convert my insurance program to a source of new money?
- Do I have adequate health and accident insurance?
- Do I have adequate major medical insurance?
- Do I have adequate hospital and surgical insurance?
- Do I have Dental Insurance?

Income Tax
- Am I taking all the deductions to which I am entitled?
- Am I arranging for some income to be sheltered through IRA or Keogh?
- Can I reduce my taxable income with tax exempt securities?

College Funding
- Have I transferred assets to my children under the Uniform Gifts to Minors Act?
- Is a tax-free college fund set up for my children?
- Have I given $3000 or, if my spouse agrees, $6000 to each child this year?

Property and Securities
- Am I holding any stock or property that is not growing or producing income?
- Should I take tax losses on these properties?

EXHIBIT VII. **FINANCIAL PLAN OF ACTION (Sample).**

1977

1. Have wills written for myself and wife at once!

2. Transfer 22 shares of XYZ stock (worth about $6000) to daughter under Uniform Gifts to Minors Act (UGTMA). Use least expensive shares. Appoint wife custodian.

3. Sell the shares for daughter and invest in 4-year certificates of deposit at PQR Federal Savings and Loan at 7½% interest for daughter's UGTMA account. These will mature to pay tuition for the last year of college.

4. Transfer 22 shares of XYZ stock (worth about $6000) to son under UGTMA. Use least expensive shares. Appoint wife custodian.

5. Sell the shares for son and invest in 6-year certificates of deposit at PQR Federal Savings and Loan at 7¾% interest for son's UGTMA account. These will mature to pay tuition for the last year of college.

6. Sell, donate, or otherwise dispose of resort property. The three savings are: (1) $1503.75 per year in mortgage, interest and tax payments; (2) actual cash recovered from sale—estimate $3000; and (3) tax loss recovery, long-term capital loss—½ of $6000 ($3000 × my tax rate of 39% = $1170). All these savings should be used to set up emergency fund with ABC Savings and Loan's 6% passbook savings. Total is $1503.75 per year + $3000 cash + $1170 tax savings = $5673.75 the first year.

7. Sell EFG stock and put proceeds into municipal bond fund, tax-free, no-load, since stock dividend does not pay high enough return.

8. Switch from 5¼% passbook accounts to 6% passbook accounts. Consolidate accounts as part of emergency fund.

9. Investigate if wife is eligible for retirement program through her employer. If not, set up an IRA account for her at PDQ Savings and Loan which pays 7¾% on minimum of $10 deposit, guaranteed 6 years. Estimate earnings for 1977 and put 15% in account as soon as possible. I can shelter IRA for whole year—even before the money is actually earned—if it works out by December 31, 1977. I get a whopping tax saving and tax sheltered interest.

10. DEF Bank and Trust offers day-of-deposit, day-of-withdrawal interest on savings. Shift my checking account there. Make all deposits to savings and have regular transfers from savings to checking. Monday is a good day to effect the transfers since I get benefit of weekend interest. Keep $300 in savings, and checking is free. This added interest adds up, without reducing my checking account flexibility.

1978

1. Transfer 22 more shares of XYZ stock (another $6000) to daughter under UGTMA.

2. Sell the shares for daughter. Buy 6¾%, 2½-year certificates of deposit for second and third years of college tuition.

3. Transfer 22 more shares of XYZ stock (another $6000) to son under UGTMA.

4. Sell the shares for son. Buy 7½%, 4-year certificates of deposit for first years of college.

5. Continue to buy company stock on the stock purchase plan in order to receive 15% company contribution. Sell the stock when enough accumulates to buy discount municipal bonds, creating both tax-free income and capital appreciation. Buy my own state's or Puerto Rico bonds since they are free of both federal and state tax.

6. When insurance premium comes due, investigate cashing in my policy to buy tax-free municipals. Must make sure I have qualified for and acquired the net needed amount of term insurance. By 1989 I will have $10,000 in hand without having to die for it.

7. Roll over my maturing 6% certificate of deposit to a 7¾%, 6-year certificate.

1979

1. Transfer 15 more shares of XYZ stock to daughter (about $4100) under UGTMA.

2. Sell the shares for daughter. Deposit in 6% passbook account to pay early schooling requirements.

3. Transfer 15 more shares of XYZ stock to son (about $4100) under UGTMA.

4. Sell the shares for son. Buy 7½%, 4-year certificates of deposit for middle years of college tuition.

5. Continue to buy discount municipal bonds maturing in medium term.

6. As municipal bonds mature, roll them over into higher yielding par bonds, preparing for retirement income.

1980 to Retirement

1. Continue municipal bond purchases.

2. Continue rolling over bonds to higher yields.

First 4 years after retirement

1. Sell off ¼ of my XYZ stock per year (50–70 shares, depending on retirement date). Invest in high-yield municipals or in high-return stocks— utilities, or whatever is hot at the time (but no speculative stock issues). The capital gain bite on about $100 per share (½ of $5000 × tax rate of 28% = $1400) is not that hard to swallow.

8. Getting professional help when you need it

No book, no guide, no manual will have all the answers to any subject. There are always questions that are not answered. That's why there are professionals in a variety of fields ready to help you with your plans and ideas. Some of this outside help will be free; some will cost you money. The point is, if you're uncertain about a step in your Plan of Action, rather than do something that cannot be undone, ask for help.

This book provides wide guidelines and suggestions. It helps you with the organization of your affairs for retirement and the production of a Plan of Action. However, the legality, taxability, and current validity of any approach frequently changes, and major financial steps should be carefully investigated.

The cost of services will vary considerably:

The cost of advice

Professional	Cost of Advice
Attorney	Discuss fee; some states allow advertising
Investment Advisor	Usually free; makes money on your security transactions
Accountant	Discuss fee; some advertise fees
Banking Institution	Usually free, but may charge for a variety of services
Insurance Agent	Usually free; makes commission on business done with you
Company Personnel Department	Free; may not be willing or allowed to give opinions on financial alternatives
Social Security Administration	Free

Professional services are often competitive, so shop around for the best deal. This includes fees, interest rates paid for your money, interest rates charged for you to borrow, cost for services (free checking, free traveler's checks, free gifts, etc.), charges for commissions on stocks or bonds, and so forth.

The following table indicates some situations where professionals can help.

TABLE X. **KINDS OF HELP YOU CAN GET.**

Professional	Advice on:
Attorney	Wills for husband and wife Questions on legality of transactions (i.e., borrowing on home equity) Uniform Gifts to Minors — rules and regulations
Investment Advisor	Stocks and stock options Bonds — corporate, municipal and "flower" U.S. securities Uniform Gifts to Minors — securities transfer IRA/Keogh investments Municipal bond funds (but you'll have to check no-loads yourself)
Accountant	Income tax returns Deductions Estate planning Pension transferability regulations Consequences of gifts over $3000 on estates (Uniform Gifts to Minors) Refinancing or second mortgage interest deductibility
Banking Institutions	Safe deposit box Savings/checking account — day-of-deposit, day-of-withdrawal savings IRA/Keogh accounts Uniform Gifts to Minors — savings account December U.S. Savings Bonds Series E — redemption value tables Certificates of deposit (savings certificates) Converting E bonds to H bonds Mortgage financing evaluations
Insurance Agent	Term insurance Annuities and retirement income insurance Cash surrender values of current policies Paid up insurance "Umbrella" liability policy Health, accident, major medical, hospital, and surgical insurance

Company Personnel Department
Retirement Program
Company insurance
"Joint and survivor" options
Vacation deferral policy
Health and dental insurance after retirement
Major medical benefits after retirement
Life insurance after retirement
E bond payroll deductions
Stock purchase plan
Credit unions, and life insurance available through them

Social Security Administration
Social Security numbers for your children
Request for "statement of wages"
Applying for benefits
Current retirement benefits
Earnings you can make without losing benefits

9. Increasing retirement income

This chapter is going to assume that you are now "officially" retired. (Enjoy the feeling while it lasts!) Your two biggest asset boosters—time and compound interest—have run out. You are now at the point where you must live off resources that exist at this moment. The name of the game, from the end of this sentence on, is I-N-C-O-M-E!

Principles for retirement income

Investment during retirement still requires the same principles of safety, liquidity, and return that we discussed in Chapter 5. In retirement, return and safety are especially important since you *must* live off the return, and it *must* continue without interruption or loss because you have little time to recoup a loss.

Liquidity becomes somewhat less important unless you have some known need for a large amount of cash at some specific time. This means you can tie up assets for longer periods of time in order to receive higher returns. High income sources offering considerable safety include:

- Common stocks with histories of long-time dividend payment and high yields
- Preferred stocks of high quality and yield
- Corporate bonds of high quality companies
- Bond funds of both corporations and municipalities
- Certificates of deposit
- U. S. Government securities
- Municipal bonds

Most of these are fixed income securities, with the exception of common stocks. Because of the unpredictability of the money and economic markets, a balanced portfolio is generally useful. You want a certain amount of money due regularly for reinvestment in order to take advantage of upward fluctuations in interest rates, but not so much that a lower interest rate will hurt you severely.

Let's look at these potential investments from the standpoint of the minimum cost that it takes to acquire them.

High-Income, Safe-Return Investments

FOR $1000 OR LESS

U. S. Treasury notes: Denominations of $1000, $5000, $10,000, $100,000 and up. Issued from one-to 10-year term; pay interest with semi-annual coupons. Notes are offered at auction when the Treasury refinances. Return in early 1977 was about 4½% to 7½%. Federally taxable, but exempt from state taxes.

U. S. Series H bonds: Denominations of $100, $500, $1000 and up. Issued for 10 years, but extended indefinitely. Pay interest by Treasury check semi-annually. Return in late 1977 was 6%. Federally taxable, but exempt from state taxes. Series E bonds can be "rolled over" into H's without tax liability.

U. S. Government agency securities: Federal Land Bank bonds—minimum purchase $1000; rates in early 1977 were between 5% and 7½%. Maturities range from 30 days to 15 years.

Savings certificates: Savings certificates are issued by banks, savings and loan associations, saving funds, etc. Many institutions offer a range of yields and maturities for a minimum purchase of $1000. Typical of late 1977 offerings are the following:

Rate	Period Must Be Held	(Basic Period)
6½%	12 months to 23 months	(1 yr)
6¾%	24 months to 35 months	(2 yrs)
7%	36 months to 47 months	(3 yrs)
7½%	48 months to 71 months	(4 yrs)
7¾%	72 months to 96 months	(6 yrs)

Interest on certificates can be paid monthly or quarterly by check to the holder. If money is withdrawn before maturity, one quarter's interest is lost as a penalty, and all other interest received drops back to the institution's passbook rate (5–6%). This penalty can be itemized as a tax deduction.

Unit investment trusts: Diversified portfolios of specific types of securities. Some invest only in corporate bonds, some in municipal bonds, others in preferred stocks. Trusts pay income monthly or semi-annually, providing good diversification for a small investment. Returns vary considerably in the 4–8% range.

FOR $1000–5000
Municipal bond funds: Many new funds of this nature have sprung up since late 1976, when the funds were allowed to pass federal tax exemption on the income to the individual fund investor. As of early 1977, at least six no-load (that is, carrying no sales charge) municipal funds were organized. Most require a $1000–2500 minimum investment and earn about 5–6% tax free. You can arrange a regular income to be paid monthly or quarterly. Some issue blank checks which you can fill out to pay bills of over $500; the fund automatically cashes your shares to pay the bill. A partial list of such funds include:

- Dreyfus Tax Exempt Bond Fund, Inc., 600 Madison Ave., New York, NY 10022
- Federated Tax-Free Income Fund, Inc., P.O. Box 1912, Boston, MA 02105
- Fidelity Municipal Bond Fund, Inc., P.O. Box 193, Boston, MA 02101
- Oppenheimer Tax Free Bond Fund, Inc., One New York Plaza, New York, NY 10004
- Rowe Price Tax-Free Income Fund, Inc., 100 E. Pratt St., Baltimore, MD 21202
- Scudder Municipal Bond Fund, Inc. 10 Port Office Square, Boston, MA 02109

Municipal bonds: The usual minimum bond order is $5000 face value which would generally buy one new issue $5000 bond. Discount bonds would cost less. As discussed in Chapter 5, there are marked variables in the bond market. In early 1977, new issues of bonds were selling with tax-free returns like this:

AAA	4½ — 5¼%
AA	5 — 5½%
A	5¼ — 5¾%
BAA	5½ — 6¼%

The term of these bonds is usually 5–50 years; some are "callable" after 10–15 years; all are federal tax exempt and usually state tax exempt in the home state of issue. Most municipals are unregistered "bearer" bonds (that is, payable to whoever presents the bond for cashing), and therefore require security of storage. Coupons are clipped and cashed semi-annually. Since issues come out every month of the year, purchasing 6 bonds ($30,000 face value), can provide a monthly income of about $150 tax free.

U. S. Government agency securities: Federal Intermediate Credit Bank debentures, Federal Home Loan Bank debentures, debentures from banks for cooperatives, TVA notes, and Farm Credit Bank discount notes are all issued in $5000 denominations. Most trade at discount on a yield basis. In early 1977 they paid 5–7%.

Utility stocks: Many utilities with long-time dividend paying records are selling at prices where the dividends pay a good return. The utility stocks as a group were adversely affected by the fuel crisis in the mid-1970s, even though their earnings and prospects remained good. These stocks should remain good values unless fixed income security interest rates rise sharply. A few prices and returns on investment in early 1977 were:

Utility	Price	Dividend	Yield	Cost of 100 Shares (plus commissions)
Cincinnati Gas & Electric	22-1/2	$1.64	7.29%	$2250
Commonwealth Edison	30-3/8	$2.40	7.9%	$3038
Consolidated Edison	21-5/8	$2.00	8.82%	$2168
Consumer Power	22-3/8	$2.00	8.94%	$2238
Detroit Edison	15-5/8	$1.45	9.25%	$1568
Florida Power	30-1/4	$2.28	7.54%	$3025
Kansas City Power & Light	29-3/4	$2.36	7.93%	$2975
Philadelphia Electric	18-1/4	$1.64	8.9%	$1825
Virginia Electric Power Co.	15-1/8	$1.24	8.2%	$1513
Wisconsin Gas	20-1/4	$1.70	8.4%	$2025

Preferred stocks: In early 1977, preferred's were returning 8–9.5% on investment. There are so many of these stocks, offered mostly by utilities, that you will need the professional help of your broker to pick the ones that are right for you.

Corporate bonds: Minimum order is usually $5000 for one new issue corporate bond. Corporate bonds often yield a percentage point to three points more than an equally rated municipal bond, but of course the yield is not tax exempt. The history of corporate bonds abounds with "called" issues, refinanced as interest rates fall. Corporations are more likely to refinance an issue than are municipalities.

Thrift certificates: Obligations of financial organizations—often in the consumer finance business—whose principal business is making direct loans to individuals, purchasing retail sales contracts, and providing related insurance contracts. The thrift certificate is usually neither insured nor guaranteed by any lien on the assets of the issuing company, nor is it supported by sinking fund provisions. The companies are not regulated banks or savings and loan associations, but private financial corporations operating under state and federal laws. Since they issue unsecured obligations, their risk is high, but as a result they pay an extremely attractive return ranging from 6½% for "demand" certificates to over 9¼% for 4–6 year certificates. Minimum investment ranges from $500 to $5000, depending on term and interest rate. An example of such certificates are those issued by First Pennsylvania Financial Services, Inc., of Philadelphia. There is generally no trading market for these certificates, and there are no commissions or charges to pay. Interest is usually paid semi-annually, or it can be retained and compounded. The higher denomination certificates can be arranged to provide a monthly income. All interest is taxable under federal, state, and local income tax laws.

FOR $10,000

U. S. Treasury bills: Obligations that mature in 3, 6, or 12 months are sold at auction weekly or monthly. The early 1977 auction rate was based on a 4.5–5.3% return. Federally taxable, but exempt from state taxes. These bills trade on a discount basis. You buy them for less than face value and the U.S. Treasury redeems them for full face value at maturity.

U. S. Government agency securities: Federal National Mortgage Association (FNMA) debentures and discount notes (called "Fannie-Mae's" for short) issued in $10,000 minimum denominations, trade at discount on a yield basis. Interest is paid by coupon. Maturities range from 30 days to 15 years. Interest was 4½–7% in early 1977.

FOR $25,000

Government National Mortgage Association securities: Certificates of ownership for a portfolio of mortgages. GNMA guarantees the mortgages in the portfolio and also the interest and principal on the certificates. "Ginnie Mae's," as they are nicknamed, provide monthly checks and a fairly large cash flow which includes both interest and return of principal. Interest rates hover around 6%–8%. Some GNMA mutual funds offer GNMA's for more modest amounts than $25,000.

Certificates of deposit: Offer negotiable interest rates.

Commercial paper: Short-term promissory notes; up to nine months. Used to fill short-term corporate needs.

Banker's acceptances: Another short-term draft resulting from some banking transaction; up to nine months.

Money market funds: These deal in certificates of deposit, commercial paper, and banker's acceptances. This will provide you with liquidity, flexible management, and as high yields as are possible from this type of investment. Further, the minimum investment is often less than $5000. Some of the no-load money market funds are listed below. In early 1977, they were yielding a little over 5%.

- Anchor Daily Income Fund, Westminster St. at Parker, Elizabeth, NJ 07207
- Dreyfus Liquid Assets, 600 Madison Ave., New York, NY 10022
- Fidelity Daily Income Trust, P.O. Box 832, Boston, MA 02103
- Money Market Management, 421 Seventh Ave., Pittsburgh, PA 15219
- Oppenheimer Monetary Bridge, One New York Plaza, New York, NY 10004
- Pro Income Inc., Valley Forge, PA 19481
- The Reserve Fund, 1301 Sixth Avenue, New York, NY 10019
- Scudder Managed Reserves, 10 Port Office Square, Boston, MA 02109
- Kemper Money Market, 120 LaSalle St., Chicago, IL 60603

FOR $100,000

More Speculative Investments

SELLING "COVERED" OPTIONS

Another game, not for the chicken-hearted, is selling options. If you have 100 shares of a popular common stock on which you have a gain, you can sell an option to a purchaser to buy your stock at a specific price at a specific time. This "covered" option commits you to sell the stock for the option price *if* the person who paid you the option premium "calls" his option at the specified time. The worst eventuality would be that you would have to deliver the stock, keeping (1) the option premium as well as (2) the option price per share as your return. The best outcome would be that your stock, at the time the option becomes valid, would be selling for less than the option price, and therefore would *probably* not be "called." in this case, you would keep your stock *and* keep the option premium.

Your risk is that the price of your stock would rise substantially above the option price. You would not be able to sell your stock for its true value until the option period ran out. In all probability, you would never receive its true value, since the option purchaser would promptly "call" your stock at the appointed time.

Option selling is not for novices. The technique should be approached with caution and, even then, only with expert help from your broker. It is not a sure thing.

"NAKED" OPTIONS ARE A NO-NO

Never get involved in selling "naked" options—options you sell without owning the stock. This can be a disaster if the stock price rises, since you will be legally bound to buy the stock on the market at its higher price at the option time and sell it immediately at the lower option price. That's a no-win proposition; no one ever made money by "buying high and selling low."

HOW OPTIONS WORK

Let's look at an example of how options work. In late January of 1977, the option market for International Telephone and Telegraph (ITT) looked like this:

Option Price	1/26/77 Market Price	Feb. Option	May Option	Aug. Option
$25	$34.25	$9.25	No Option Available	
$30	$34.25	$4.375	$4.75	$5.25
$35	$34.25	$1.00	$1.75	$2.25

This means that for a premium of $9.25 per share, you would sell rights to buy 100 shares of your ITT stock for $25 per share to be exercised in February, 1977. As an option seller, you would be sure of getting $25 per share for your stock plus $9.25 per share for the option, or $34.25 on a stock trading in January at $34.25 per share. The buyer-seller contention is that you as a seller hope the price goes *down* so that the buyer will not exercise the option to buy your stock. You would keep the stock and pocket the $9.25 per share. If, on the other hand, the stock goes up to, say $40, you could not sell at that price, but would be obliged to sell at the agreed upon $25 per share. You would still keep the $9.25 option price, however.

The likelihood of an option being exercised is a function of the share cost plus the option cost. Using the same tables, the combined option price plus option premium would have to be exceeded by the market price of the stock in order for the buyer to break even on executing the option to buy. This is illustrated as follows:

Option Price	Market price that must be exceeded for options in:		
	February	May	August
$25	$34.25	No Option Available	
$30	$34.375	$34.75	$35.25
$35	$36.00	$36.75	$37.25

Liquidity, emergency reserves, and investment reserves

If you're retired, how much liquidity should you have? Well, as in your working days, you need *emergency reserves* made up of highly liquid assets. They should represent three months of earnings and can be made up of passbook savings funds, the cash value of insurance, U.S. Savings Bonds, or money market or municipal bond funds. These are all highly liquid investments whose value will not vary much with the fluctuations of a stock market or outside interest rates, or become diminished by cost penalties for early surrender.

Your *investment reserves* should be made up of funds which are not needed for living expenses. They can include:
- Interest
- Dividends from investments
- Regular savings
- Tax savings

Clearly, in retirement, investment reserves may be quite small since you are depending on investment income to live. However, in some cases, as illustrated by Exhibit I in Chapter 2, if your expense and income projections are correct, you should have some money for investment reserves by age 65, and even more by age 69. Your own Retirement Plan will help you determine what your investment reserves may be, and at what age you can expect the funds to become available.

The row over mandatory retirement

In 1976, 90% of all those entering claims for retirement benefits with the Social Security Administration were younger than age 65.

Not everyone objects to this development. Former United Auto Workers president, Leonard Woodcock, has been quoted as saying, "The problems related to mandatory retirement are not of major concern to us because the workers we represent have a far greater interest in early, rather than late retirement...." A spokesman for the AFL-CIO recently stated, "This is mostly an upper class thing. It's the professionals and executives who might not want to retire. The blue-collar employee generally doesn't want to keep working...."

So what's the big fuss? The problem is the word "mandatory." The notion of edicting an age at which you *must* retire has become, for some folks, a rallying cry. The charge is made that denying a job to a person because of age is discriminatory.

What are the pros and cons of mandatory retirement? Let's look at some of the issues.

Pro   There are already too few jobs for young people; eliminating mandatory retirement would make the situation even worse.

Con   Two wrongs don't make a right; there shouldn't be discrimination against either young or old workers. The economy should be able to expand to provide jobs for all.

Pro   The older worker is less efficient and often is paid higher salaries than a younger worker. It would be difficult to dismiss an older worker since it might seem that salary was the reason. Discharging the older worker would also be difficult because of loyalty to the employee or because of fear that the discharged employee would bring a lawsuit.

Con   Each person, regardless of age, should be evaluated on the ability to perform his or her job. Only when people can no longer do the work should their company tell them so.

Pro   Most pension systems are designed around a mandatory retirement concept, and a discontinuance of mandatory retirement would badly interfere with the fiscal integrity of these funds.

Con   Certainly in the short run there would be a *positive* effect on pension funds if fewer people were drawing retirement pay. The combination of less demand, coupled with more contributions, should improve pension fund viability, rather than hurt it. In addition, if workers retired at a later age, actuarially, they would not be drawing a pension as long; the number of years they would be expected to live would be less.

Pro   The only reason Social Security wants to extend the retirement age is to ease the demand on Social Security resources. Any such extension would only be a stop-gap since the ratio of workers supporting a retiree has dropped from 7:1 in 1935 to 3.2:1 today. By the year 2025, that ratio will be 2:1. There is no way the present system can continue without infusions of general Treasury cash.

Perhaps, but the choice is onerous. Consider that most people pay more in Social Security payments than they do in income tax, and that today employers match these contributions dollar for dollar. Increasing the age of eligibility is certainly better than raising taxes again or reducing Social Security benefits. *Con*

More and more people are interested in retiring earlier, not later. Consider the following chart: *Pro*

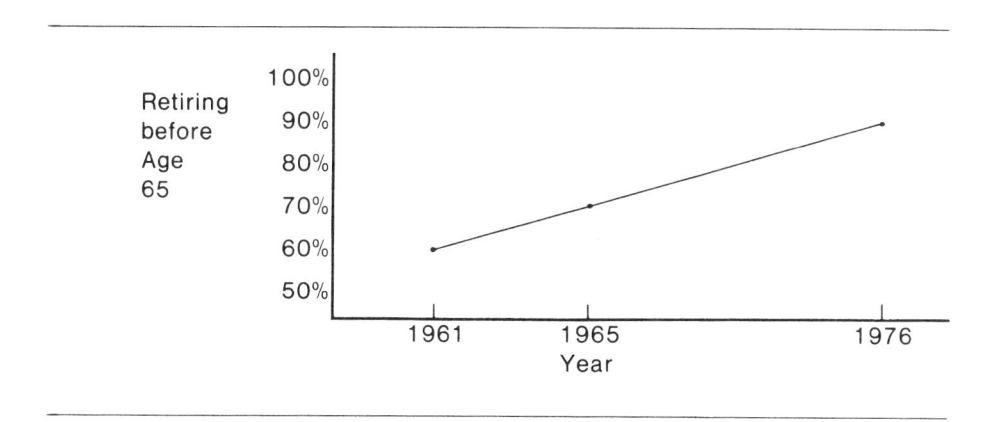

[Chart: Retiring before Age 65, showing rising trend from 60% in 1961 to 70% in 1965 to 90% in 1976]

Extending this projection indicates that by 1981, nearly 100% of workers would want to retire early.

This only proves the point—the effect of making retirement voluntary would be negligible on the economy since the number of workers staying on the job beyond age 65 would be very small. Why not give these few the right to choose when they should retire, assuming they are physically and mentally able to do their job? *Con*

All you're doing is putting the onus of retiring older workers on management. How do you tell an old, faithful employee he's had it? This would tear up his ego, and he would be resentful of his employer—possibly of his own life's productiveness as well. *Pro*

Experience has shown that it's a lot easier to tell an older person he isn't carrying his share than it is to tell a younger person. Older employees tend to be more critical of their own performance than is management. Assuming there is a reasonable retirement program to migrate to, they would more likely offer to retire voluntarily. *Con*

Pro If we are truly going to have a system free of age discrimination and based strictly on performance, we may find that a worker is "burnt out" at age 50. How do we tell him he should retire, especially if the company retirement system is not structured to begin at that age?

Con You have a point. I guess the system should be restructured to reflect ability to perform, and retirement could theoretically begin any time after vesting, obviously at lower pension amounts. On the other hand, you could reassign that worker to a job he could successfully handle; but that would be no different than the option that management has today.

And so the controversy rages. The "con" argument has been gaining ground since in 1977 Congress increased the mandatory retirement age to 70. However, regardless of the outcome, mandatory retirement or voluntary, you will retire sometime. The needs of retirees are basically the same—they must be able to retire with dignity and self-respect. Obviously, what you do in your retirement years must satisfy the inner person. With the principles discussed in this book, that inner person can be well fed, comfortably housed, and free to enjoy his or her declining years.

So plan your own retirement—it will last you the rest of your life.

Appendix

Tables and worksheets

The following tables and forms are for your use in planning your own retirement.

TABLE A is a listing of the before-tax effective rate of interest when compounded quarterly, monthly, and daily. Depending on the savings institution, you can approximate how your money will grow using these tables. For periods longer than five or six years, it becomes tiresome to multiply a given sum with a percentage for each year, so TABLES B and C, which only use annual compounding, can be used to approximate long-term growth.

TABLE B shows what would happen to $1 at various interest rates over various periods of time. You can easily see the "rule of 72" at work here. Notice the number of years it takes to:

	5%	6%	7%	8%	9%	10%
Double	14+	12	10+	9	8	7+
Quadruple	28+	24	20+	18	16+	14+
Octuple	42+	36	30	27	24+	21+

TABLE C shows how $1 added each year and accumulated with compound interest grows at various interest rates over time. You can amass over $100,000 by saving $20 per week as follows:

Reaches $100,000	26%	7%	8%	9%	10%
in this many years:	33	30	28	26	25

TABLE D is the new combination estate and gift tax-rate schedule effective January 1, 1977. The rates actually go higher than the $2,000,000 listed on the table, but since I don't know anybody with that

101

kind of money, I guess it goes far enough. If not, you can get the rest of the table rates from your friendly IRS office, or the Treasury's Estate and Gift Tax Division.

The three blank worksheets at the back of the book are copies of the example Exhibits in the book. You can use these worksheets when planning your own retirement.

To develop your "First Cut" and "Smoothed-out" Retirement Plans get some 16-column journal pages from a local business-forms stationer. These pages will allow you to create columns for every intervening year between the present and your anticipated date of retirement and beyond.

TABLE A. EFFECTIVE RATES OF COMPOUND INTEREST.

Actual Yearly Rate	Compound Quarterly	Compound Monthly	Compound Daily
8%	8.24%	8.299%	8.44%
7¾%	7.98	8.031	8.17
7½	7.71	7.76	7.90
7¼	7.45	7.49	7.625
7	7.19	7.23	7.36
6¾	6.92	6.96	7.08
6½	6.66	6.696	6.81
6¼	6.40	6.43	6.54
6	6.14	6.17	6.275
5¾	5.875	5.90	6.00
5½	5.61	5.64	5.73
5¼	5.35	5.38	5.47
5	5.09	5.12	5.20

TABLE B. COMPOUNDED AMOUNT ON $1.00 AT VARIOUS INTEREST RATES.

No. of Years	\multicolumn{6}{c}{Rate of Interest}
	5%	6%	7%	8%	9%	10%
1	$1.05	$1.06	$1.07	$ 1.08	$ 1.09	$ 1.10
2	1.10	1.12	1.14	1.17	1.19	1.21
3	1.16	1.19	1.22	1.26	1.30	1.33
4	1.22	1.26	1.31	1.36	1.41	1.46
5	1.28	1.34	1.40	1.47	1.54	1.61
6	$1.34	$1.42	$1.50	$ 1.59	$ 1.68	$ 1.77
7	1.41	1.50	1.61	1.71	1.83	1.95
8	1.48	1.59	1.72	1.85	1.99	2.14
9	1.55	1.69	1.84	2.00	2.17	2.36
10	1.63	1.79	1.97	2.16	2.37	2.59

TABLE B. (continued)

No. of Years	5%	6%	7%	8%	9%	10%
11	$1.71	$1.90	$2.10	$ 2.33	$ 2.58	$ 2.85
12	1.80	2.01	2.25	2.52	2.81	3.14
13	1.89	2.13	2.41	2.72	3.07	3.45
14	1.98	2.26	2.58	2.94	3.34	3.80
15	2.08	2.40	2.76	3.17	3.64	4.17
16	$2.18	$2.54	$2.95	$ 3.43	$ 3.97	$ 4.59
17	2.29	2.69	3.16	3.70	4.33	5.05
18	2.41	2.85	3.38	4.00	4.72	5.56
19	2.53	3.03	3.62	4.32	5.14	6.12
20	2.65	3.21	3.87	4.66	5.60	6.73
21	$2.78	$3.40	$4.14	$ 5.03	$ 6.11	$ 7.40
22	2.92	3.60	4.43	5.44	6.66	8.14
23	3.07	3.82	4.74	5.87	7.26	8.95
24	3.22	4.05	5.07	6.34	7.91	9.85
25	3.39	4.29	5.43	6.85	8.62	10.83
26	$3.55	$4.55	$5.81	$ 7.40	$ 9.40	$11.91
27	3.73	4.82	6.21	7.99	10.24	13.11
28	3.92	5.11	6.65	8.63	11.17	14.42
29	4.12	5.42	7.11	9.32	12.17	15.86
30	4.32	5.74	7.61	10.06	13.27	17.45

TABLE C. ACCUMULATED AMOUNT ON $1.00 DEPOSITS AT THE BEGINNING OF EACH YEAR AT VARIOUS INTEREST RATES.

No. of Years	6%	7%	8%	9%	10%
1	$ 1.06	$ 1.07	$ 1.08	$ 1.09	$ 1.10
2	2.18	2.21	2.25	2.28	2.31
3	3.37	3.44	3.51	3.57	3.64
4	4.64	4.75	4.87	4.98	5.11
5	5.98	6.15	6.34	6.52	6.72
6	$ 7.39	$ 7.65	$ 7.92	$ 8.20	$ 8.49
7	8.90	9.26	9.64	10.03	10.44
8	10.49	10.98	11.49	12.02	12.58
9	12.18	12.82	13.49	14.19	14.94
10	13.97	14.78	15.65	16.56	17.53
11	$15.87	$ 16.89	$ 17.98	$ 19.14	$ 20.38
12	17.88	19.14	20.50	21.95	23.52
13	20.02	21.55	23.22	25.02	26.97
14	22.28	24.13	26.16	28.36	30.77
15	24.67	26.89	29.33	32.00	34.95

TABLE C. (*continued*)

No. of Years	6%	7%	8%	9%	10%
			Rate of Interest		
16	$27.21	$ 29.84	$ 32.76	$ 35.97	$ 39.54
17	29.91	33.00	36.46	40.30	44.60
18	32.76	36.38	40.45	45.02	50.16
19	35.79	40.00	44.77	50.16	56.27
20	38.99	43.87	49.42	55.76	63.00
21	$42.39	$ 48.01	$ 54.45	$ 61.87	$ 70.40
22	46.00	52.44	59.89	68.53	78.54
23	49.82	57.18	65.76	75.79	87.50
24	53.86	62.25	72.10	83.70	97.35
25	58.16	67.68	78.95	92.32	108.18
26	$62.71	$ 73.49	$ 86.35	$101.72	$120.10
27	67.53	79.70	94.34	111.97	133.21
28	72.64	86.35	102.97	123.13	147.63
29	78.06	93.46	112.28	135.30	163.49
30	83.80	101.08	122.34	148.57	180.94

TABLE D. **ESTATE AND GIFT TAX RATE TABLE** (any state inheritance taxes paid are credited against any federal estate taxes due).

Estate Size After Marital Deduction Column A	Estate Tax	Plus % on Excess Of Column A
$ 100,000	$ 23,800	30%
150,000	38,800	32
250,000	70,800	34
500,000	155,800	37
750,000	248,300	39
1,000,000	345,800	41
1,250,000	448,300	43
1,500,000	555,800	45
2,000,000	780,800	49

The marital deduction has been increased to $250,000, or half the estate, whichever is greater. The exemption on inherited estates rises as follows:

Year	Estate Size	Estate Tax Credit Amount	%Tax Paid on on Next Dollar
1977	$120,666	$30,000	30%
1978	134,000	34,000	30%
1979	147,333	38,000	30%
1980	161,563	42,500	32%
1981	175,625	47,000	32%

The exemption is really in the form of an estate tax credit. This means that the first dollar beyond the exemption amount is socked with the appropriate rate on the table. For example, in 1981, the tax on a $180,000 taxable estate would be about $1400 (32% of $4,375), less any state death tax credit.

Most of the complicated gift tax/estate tax ploys that had to be calculated are now by the board since, from 1976 on, all gifts except for a $3000-per-year per person exclusion are counted in the total estate.

Highlights of The Employee Retirement Income Security Act of 1974 (ERISA)

At this writing, the most recent legislation in regard to retirement and pensions was signed into law in September 1974. The law was so voluminous and comprehensive in scope that it is still being interpreted. It attempts to standardize pension rights provisions in eight key areas. One of the immediate results of ERISA was a considerable fallout in qualified pension plans. Many employers were unable to meet the provisions of the law, so they turned the proceeds of their pension fund assets back to employees, suggesting that they roll this money into their own Individual Retirement Accounts (IRA). (See the Chapter 1 discussion of "Investment for Assured Retirement Income.")

The key areas addressed are:
- A. Qualification of the plan
- B. Eligibility of employees
- C. Vested retirement rights
- D. Funding of the plan
- E. Portability of benefits
- F. Annual benefits
- G. Plan termination insurance
- H. Reporting provisions

A. QUALIFICATION OF THE PLAN

● Must be approved by U.S. Department of Labor for disclosure, fiduciary standards, and plan termination insurance. The Department has certain intervention rights.

- The U. S. Department of the Treasury is the regulatory authority for vesting, funding, participation, and tax provisions.
- The plan must meet vesting, funding, and other standards (except for executive deferred compensation plans).
- ERISA preempts state laws on the subject.
- The effective date for established retirement plans is December 31, 1975, or later, if bargaining agreements are still in effect. Any new retirement plan is covered in the plan year after enactment.

B. ELIGIBILITY OF EMPLOYEES
- Normally, age 25 and one year of service.
- For plans with immediate vesting, age 25 and 3 years of service.
- Employees hired within 5 years of normal retirement or older may be excluded in a defined benefit plan.

C. VESTED RETIREMENT RIGHTS
- Can't be taken away regardless if fired, quit, laid off, etc.
- Schedule of vesting options (generally disregards service before age 22):

    Option 1. 100% vested after 10 years service.

    Option 2. 25% vested after 5 years service, then 5% per year for the next 5 years, then 10% per year for the next 5 years.

Years of Service	% Vested
5	25%
6	30%
7	35%
8	40%
9	45%
10	50%
11	60%
12	70%
13	80%
14	90%
15	100%

   Option 3. Uses rule of 45–50% vested when age reached plus years of service equals 45 (5 years service required), then 10% per year thereafter, with a minimum of 50% vested after 10 years service.

Minimum Vesting of 50%		*100% Vested*
Age	**Years of Service**	**Age**
40 or more	5	45
39	6	44
38	7	43
37	8	42
36	9	41
35 or less	10	40 or less

Option 4. Profit sharing plans.
- Must vest each year's contribution 100% within 5 years of the year it is made.
- Benefit accrual options as defined in the plan, provided that:

  For Option 1 — No future accrual rate can exceed any preceding future accrual rate by more than 33-1/3%.

  For Option 2 — Cumulative annual accruals at least 3% of maximum benefit for each year of service, calculated from earliest entry to retirement date.

  For Option 3 — Accrued benefit based on projected pension at current average earnings of an individual times a ratio of actual to potential years of service.
- Retirement age is not to exceed age 65 or 10 years service (whichever is later).

D. FUNDING OF THE PLAN

- Accrued unfunded liability on the effective date of the law must be funded within 40 years.
- New plans must be funded within 30 years.
- Plan amendments resulting in increases must be funded within 30 years.
- Experience gains and losses must be funded within a 15-year period.
- If a plan is funded by multiple employers, 40 years is allowed for funding and 20 years for experience gains and losses.
- All assets of the pension fund should be valued using a reasonable actuarial method that takes into account fair market value. Bonds may be carried at amortized value.

E. PORTABILITY
OF BENEFITS

- Transfers to and from Individual Retirement Accounts are permitted.
- Benefits *may* be carried from employer to employer, but this is not mandatory. (Very few plans have incorporated this benefit.)

F. ANNUAL
BENEFITS
(MAXIMUMS
ALLOWED)

- Defined benefit plans, lesser of:
Option 1 — 100% of highest 3-year average annual earnings.
Option 2 — $75,000.
Minimum of $10,000 permitted, prorated for less than 10 years service. Actuarial adjustments for employee contributions and annuity forms other than life only (joint and survivor excepted).
- Defined Contribution Plans, lesser of:
Option 1 — 25% of annual earnings.
Option 2 — $25,000.
Limit includes employer contributions, forfeitures, and a portion of employee contributions if they exceed 6% of annual earnings. Percentage utilizations of defined benefit and defined contribution limits cannot exceed 140%. Joint and survivor benefit required. May be actuarially reduced based on age of the non-covered spouse or survivor. Coverage must start for active employees at the earliest retirement age.

G. PLAN
TERMINATION
INSURANCE

- Generally paid by employer to insure benefits to current and vested employees.
- Insures vested pension benefits up to a maximum. Ancillary benefits (insurance, hospitalization, surgical, etc.) can be guaranteed if deemed insurable.
- Maximum benefit insured is the actuarial equivalent of an annuity at age 65, equal to 100% of highest 5-year average monthly pay, with a maximum of $750 per month ($9000 per year) adjusted as the Social Security wage base changes.
- Normally excludes insurance of profit-sharing and money purchase plans.
- Benefits and benefit improvements are covered after being phased in at the rate of 20% for each year the company has offered the benefit. Therefore, a benefit change, effective 5 years before, would be fully covered.
- The employer's liability is calculated up to 30% of net worth. The employer can buy liability insurance privately, or, if it's not available, from the government.

- The premium for "plan termination insurance" is $1 per participant for the first year. In the second year, the premium would be the same, or derived from a formula taking unfunded liabilities into account. In the third year and beyond, the insurance company can revise the formula subject to limits.

H. REPORTING PROVISIONS

- Actuarial reports must be filed periodically for defined benefit plans with the federal government.
- Reports must be furnished to employees periodically on the financial status of benefit plans.

BRIEF GLOSSARY OF TERMS

To help you understand some of the words and phrases used, this brief glossary may help:

Accrual basis — an accounting method where income and expense are recorded in the fiscal period in which income is earned or expenses are incurred.

Amortization — Systematic reduction of a debt by equal periodic payments sufficient to pay current interest and principal within a specified period of time.

Unfunded prior service costs — Costs arising from retirement plan improvements and associated with employee's years of service prior to the dates of plan improvement.

Pooled funds — Groups of assets managed by a bank which sells units in the entire fund to trust accounts managed by the bank.

CONFIDENTIAL

Personal Resources Record (Worksheets)

Date First Completed _____

Dates Reviewed _____ _____

_____ _____ _____

_____ _____ _____

Review with my spouse and executor after completion.

PERSONAL AND FAMILY DATA

    Me and my spouse

Name _____ Social Security No. _____

Date of birth _____ Place of birth _____

Name of spouse _____ Social Security No. _____

Date of birth _____ Place of birth _____

Date of marriage _____ Place of marriage _____

Location of marriage & birth certificates _____

    Our Children

1. Name _____ Social Security No. _____

   Date of birth _____ Place of birth _____

2. Name _____ Social Security No. _____

   Date of birth _____ Place of birth _____

3. Name _____ Social Security No. _____

   Date of birth _____ Place of birth _____

4. Name _____ Social Security No. _____

   Date of birth _____ Place of birth _____

5. Name _____ Social Security No. _____

   Date of birth _____ Place of birth _____

Location of birth certificates for children _____

Date of any previous marriage _____ Date marriage terminated _____

Name of former spouse _____

Place where marriage terminated _____

Location of property settlement or divorce decree _____

Date of Naturalization (if not born a U.S. citizen) _____

Place of Naturalization _____

Location of Naturalization records _____

IMPORTANT NAMES AND ADDRESSES

A. Medical practitioners who have records of physical history.

    Physician: _____ Address _____

    _____ Telephone _____

    Dentist: _____ Address _____

    _____ Telephone _____

    Optical: _____ Address _____

    _____ Telephone _____

B. Attorney: _____ Address _____

    _____ Telephone _____

C. Accountant: _____ Address _____

    _____ Telephone _____

D. Stock Broker _____ Address _____

    Account No. _____ Telephone _____

E. Trustee _____ Address _____

    _____ Telephone _____

F. Insurance Agents: Life _____

    Address _____ Telephone _____

    Automobile _____ Address _____

    Household goods _____ Address _____

    Health & Accident _____ Address _____

    Hospitalization _____ Address _____

    Property _____ Address _____

    Major Medical _____ Address _____

Travel _____   Address _____

Medical & Surgical _____   Address _____

Liability Insurance _____   Address _____

LEGAL MATTERS

1. I have ☐ have not ☐ executed a Will.

   Location of Will _____

   Date of Will _____ Prepared by _____

   Address _____

   My executor is _____ Address _____

   Guardians for my minor children are:

   1. Name _____ Address _____

   2. Name _____ Address _____

   Other members in family having a Will

   A. Name _____ Location _____

   Date of Will _____ Prepared by _____

   Address _____

   Executor _____ Address _____

   B. Name _____ Location _____

   Date of Will _____ Prepared by _____

   Address _____

   Executor _____ Address _____

(Note: Make certain my will complies with laws of the state in which I live.)

2. I have ☐ have not ☐ established a Trust.

   Name of Trustee _____ Address _____

3. I have ☐ do not have ☐ a safety deposit box.

   Location _____

   Box No. _____ Location of key _____

Person(s) with right to enter box.

1. _____

2. _____

3. _____

Contents of the box are _____

_____

4. Power of Attorney: ☐ I have executed a Power of Attorney.

   ☐ I have not executed a Power of Attorney.

   If Yes: Name _____ Address _____

(Note - A Power of Attorney is automatically revoked when I die.)

INFORMATION IN THE EVENT OF MY DEATH

A. Social Security

Location of my Social Security Card _____

Location of employment record showing Social Security payments _____
_____

Death benefit — $255 — Apply to nearest Social Security Office

Address _____

B. Military Service

I am ☐ am not ☐ a veteran of the U.S. Armed Forces.

I served on active duty from _____ to _____

In (branch) _____ with a rank of _____

Service Serial No. _____

My Military discharge and related papers are located _____
_____

I have ☐ have not ☐ applied to the Veterans Administration for disability rating. My

Claim Number is_____

My Rating is _____

Burial benefit — $250 — Apply to nearest Veterans Administration Office. The Government will provide a headstone or memorial marker without charge.

C. Fraternal Organizations

I am a member of the following organizations. Some may provide death benefits.

1. _____
2. _____
3. _____

D. Availability of cash to meet immediate needs

Lump sum Insurance (amount) _____ Company _____

Lump sum Social Security (amount) _____

Other funds _____

_____

(Note: Joint checking accounts not immediately usable in my state.)

E. Funeral arrangements

1. I would ☐ would not ☐ like full military honors (if a veteran).

2. I would like to be buried at:

Cemetery name _____ Address _____

3. I wish to be buried ☐ cremated ☐.

4. I do ☐ do not ☐ have a niche or lot.

Location of niche or lot _____

5. I would prefer the following mortician:

Name _____ Contact _____

Location _____

6. I have ☐ have not ☐ provided for perpetual care.

7. I would prefer flowers ☐ contribution to charity ☐.

What charity, if so desired _____

8. I strongly desire a modest service and urge limiting final expenses to

$ _____ plus grave and opening of $ _____.

9. Request undertaker to provide at least _____ copies of my Death Certificate.
(Note: Copies will be needed by each life insurance company, for real estate title transfer, government benefits, Social Security and VA, personal property and securities, stocks, bonds, vehicle registrations, etc.)

F. Persons to be notified in case of death

   1. Employer Name _____   Address _____

      _____   Telephone _____

   2. Name _____   Address _____

      _____   Telephone _____

   3. Name _____   Address _____

      _____   Telephone _____

SAVINGS AND BANKING INFORMATION

1. Type of account

    A. Savings accounts

    1. Account No. _____ Institution _____

       Location _____

       Rate of return _____ % Approximate value $ _____

    2. Account No. _____ Institution _____

       Location _____

       Rate of return _____ % Approximate value $ _____

    3. Account No. _____ Institution _____

       Location _____

       Rate of return _____ % Approximate value $ _____

    4. Account No. _____ Institution _____

       Location _____

       Rate of return _____ % Approximate value $ _____

    Location of Savings and Bank Account Books _____

    _____

    B. Checking (Indicate whether joint and with whom)

    1. Account No. _____ Institution _____

       Location _____

       Joint Name _____ Approximate Value $ _____

    2. Account No. _____ Institution _____

       Location _____

       Joint Name _____ Approximate Value $ _____

3\. Account No. _____ Institution _____

Location _____

Joint Name _____ Approximate Value $ _____

Location of Checkbooks _____

Location of cancelled checks _____

2\. Banking Institution Contacts

A. Name _____ With _____

B. Name _____ With _____

3\. Outstanding debts (including vehicles; mortgage information comes under real estate)

A. By whom held _____

Amount $ _____ Where recorded _____

If paid, location of discharge paper _____

B. By whom held _____

Amount $ _____ Where recorded _____

If paid, location of discharge paper _____

C. By whom held _____ Where recorded _____

If paid, location of discharge paper _____

SECURITIES AND INVESTMENTS

1. Bonds

   Location _____

   Approximate Value $ _____ Recommendation _____

   _____

2. Stock Certificates

   Location _____

   Approximate Value $ _____ Recommendation _____

   _____

3. Mutual Fund Shares

   Location _____

   Approximate Value $ _____ Recommendation _____

   _____

4. Bond Fund Shares

   Location _____

   Approximate Value $ _____ Recommendation _____

   _____

5. Other Investments

   Location _____

   Approximate Value $ _____ Recommendation _____

   _____

INSURANCE

1. Life Insurance

    A. On my life

        1. Type of policy _____ Amount $ _____

            Policy No. _____ Company _____

            1st beneficiary _____ Premium $ _____

            2nd beneficiary _____ Cash Value $ _____

        2. Type of policy _____ Amount $ _____

            Policy No. _____ Company _____

            1st beneficiary _____ Premium $ _____

            2nd beneficiary _____ Cash Value $ _____

        3. Type of policy _____ Amount $ _____

            Policy No. _____ Company _____

            1st beneficiary _____ Premium $ _____

            2nd beneficiary _____ Cash Value $ _____

        4. Type of policy _____ Amount $ _____

            Policy No. _____ Company _____

            1st beneficiary _____ Premium $ _____

            2nd beneficiary _____ Cash Value $ _____

    B. On my spouse's life

        1. Type of policy _____ Amount $ _____

            Policy No. _____ Company _____

            1st beneficiary _____ Premium $ _____

            2nd beneficiary _____ Cash Value $ _____

2. Type of policy _____   Amount $ _____

   Policy No. _____   Company _____

   1st beneficiary _____   Premium $ _____

   2nd beneficiary _____   Cash Value $ _____

C. On my children's lives

   1. Type of policy _____   Amount $ _____

      Policy No. _____   Company _____

      1st beneficiary _____   Premium $ _____

      2nd beneficiary _____   Cash Value $ _____

   2. Type of policy _____   Amount $ _____

      Policy No. _____   Company _____

      1st beneficiary _____   Premium $ _____

      2nd beneficiary _____   Cash Value $ _____

D. Location of policies _____
   _____

E. Any outstanding loans against policies? Which and how much?
   _____

2. Health and accident insurance

   A. Type of policy _____   Coverage _____

      Policy No. _____   Company _____

      Premium $ _____   Restrictions _____

   B. Type of policy _____   Coverage _____

      Policy No. _____   Company _____

      Premium $ _____   Restrictions _____

   C. Location of policies _____

3. Hospitalization insurance

   A. Policy No. _____ Coverage _____

   Company _____ Premium $ _____

   Address _____

   B. Policy No. _____ Coverage _____

   Company _____ Premium $ _____

   Address _____

   C. Location of policies _____

4. Vehicle Insurance (should have same coverage for each vehicle)

   Company _____ Policy No. _____

   Address _____ Premium $ _____

   Coverages:

   Fire $ _____ Theft $ _____

   Comprehensive _____ Deductible ?$ _____

   Collision _____ Deductible ?$ _____

   Medical expenses $ _____ Property damage $ _____

   Bodily injury: each person $ _____ Each Accident $ _____

   Location of Policy _____

5. Household Goods Insurance

   Company _____ Policy No. _____

   Kind of coverage _____ Amount $ _____

   Premium $ _____ Location of policy _____

6. Property Insurance

   A. Property covered: location _____

      Company _____ Policy No. _____

      Address _____ Premium $ _____

      Coverages:

         Fire $ _____ Extended coverage $ _____

         Theft $ _____ Liability $ _____

   B. Property covered: location _____

      Company _____ Policy No. _____

      Address _____ Premium $ _____

      Coverages:

         Fire $ _____ Extended coverage $ _____

         Theft $ _____ Liability $ _____

   C. Location of policies _____

   D. Personal articles floater? _____ Amount $ _____

      Premium $ _____ Location of policy _____

      Articles covered _____

7. Travel Insurance

      Company _____ Policy No. _____

      Address _____ Premium $ _____

      Coverage _____ Location of policy _____

8. Medical and Surgical Insurance

    Company _____ Policy No. _____

    Address _____ Premium $ _____

    Coverage _____ Location of policy _____

9. Major Medical Insurance

    Company _____ Policy No. _____

    Address _____ Premium $ _____

    Coverage _____ Location of policy _____

10. Dental Insurance

    Company _____ Policy No. _____

    Address _____ Premium $ _____

    Coverage _____ Location of policy _____

11. Liability Insurance (umbrella policy)

    Company _____ Policy No. _____

    Address _____ Premium $ _____

    Coverage _____ Location of policy _____

REAL ESTATE

A. Home

   Location _____

   Ownership is in my name alone ☐ I am co-owner with _____

   Title is in name of _____

   Mortgage is held by _____ Mortgage No. _____

   Address _____

   Amount of mortgage $ _____ As of _____ (date)

   Homesteaded: Yes ☐ No ☐. Assessment $_____ As of _____

   Mortgage is ☐ is not ☐ insured. Market Value $ _____

   As of _____ (date). Payments $ _____ Per month.

   Real estate taxes are ☐ are not ☐ included. Amount $ _____

   Location of Deed _____

   Where Deed is recorded _____

   Land Title _____

   Policy No. _____ Amount $ _____

   Receipts located _____

   Insurance on house: Company _____

   Mortgage paid in full and discharge recorded _____

   _____

B. Other real estate (use similar sheet for all property owned)

   Location _____

   Ownership is in my name alone ☐ I am co-owner with _____

   Title is in name of _____

129

Mortgage is held by _____ Mortgage No. _____

Address _____

Amount of mortgage $ _____ As of _____ (date)

Homesteaded: Yes ☐ No ☐. Assessment $ _____ As of _____

Mortgage is ☐ is not ☐ insured. Market Value $ _____

As of _____ (date). Payments $ _____ Per month.

Real estate taxes are ☐ are not ☐ included. Amount $ _____

Location of Deed _____

Where Deed is recorded _____

Land Title _____

Policy No. _____ Amount $ _____

Receipts located _____

Insurance on house: Company _____

Mortgage paid in full and discharge recorded _____
_____

C. Recommendations: Keep ☐ Sell ☐ Rent ☐

_____
_____
_____

PERSONAL PROPERTY

A. Vehicles

   1. Year & Make _____ Owner _____

      Identification No. _____ Market Value $ _____ As of _____

   2. Year & Make _____ Owner _____

      Identification No. _____ Market Value $ _____ As of _____

   3. Year & Make _____ Owner _____

      Identification No. _____ Market Value $ _____ As of _____

      Titles are located _____

B. Household Goods (should have separate inventory in safe place away from the house)

   1. Furniture: Approximate value $ _____

   2. Appliances and tools: Approximate value $ _____

   3. Carpets and draperies: Approximate value $ _____

   4. Jewelry and silverware: Approximate value $ _____

   5. Sports and hobby equipment: Approximate value $ _____

   6. Clothing and furs: Approximate value $ _____

   7. Paintings, books, and objets d'art: Approximate value $ _____

C. Collections

   1. Stamps: Approximate value $ _____ Where located _____

   2. Coins: Approximate value $ _____ Where located _____

   3. Other: Approximate value $ _____ Where located _____

AGREEMENTS, PARTNERSHIPS, SYNDICATES, VENTURES

(Note: Includes land purchases, investments not identified by certificates of stock, published works, etc.)

A. Approximate value $ _____   Description _____
_____

B. Approximate value $ _____   Description _____
_____

C. Approximate value $ _____   Description _____
_____

D. Approximate value $ _____   Description _____
_____

E. Approximate value $ _____   Description _____
_____

PERSONAL PAPERS

A. Location of the following:

1. Armed Forces papers (commissions, discharge, release to inactive duty, orders, transfers, etc.)
   _____

2. Income tax returns _____
   _____

3. Diplomas _____

4. Licenses _____

5. Paid bills, expense records, and canceled checks _____
   _____

6. Passports _____

7. Family health records _____
   _____

8. Other _____
   _____

B. Charge accounts and credit cards

Company	Account No.
_____	_____
_____	_____
_____	_____
_____	_____
_____	_____
_____	_____
_____	_____

Charge accounts and credit cards (continued)

Company	Account No.
_____	_____
_____	_____
_____	_____
_____	_____
_____	_____
_____	_____
_____	_____
_____	_____
_____	_____
_____	_____
_____	_____

C. Valuable papers pertaining to other persons

1. Name of person _____

    Item _____ Location _____

2. Name of person _____

    Item _____ Location _____

3. Name of person _____

    Item _____ Location _____

4. Name of person _____

    Item _____ Location _____

5. Name of person _____

    Item _____ Location _____

PERSONAL FINANCIAL STATEMENT   Date _____

Assets
Liquid (readily convertible to cash)

_____	$ _____
_____	_____
_____	_____
_____	_____
_____	_____
_____	_____
_____	_____
_____	_____
_____	_____
_____	_____
_____	_____
_____	_____
_____	_____
_____	_____
_____	_____
_____	_____
_____	_____
_____	_____
_____	_____
_____	_____
Liquid Assets	**$ _____**

Liabilities
Current (due within a year)

_____	$ _____
_____	_____
_____	_____
_____	_____
_____	_____
_____	_____
_____	_____
_____	_____
_____	_____
_____	_____
_____	_____
_____	_____
_____	_____
_____	_____
_____	_____
_____	_____
_____	_____
_____	_____
_____	_____
_____	_____
Current Liabilities	**$ _____**

Other assets (home, real estate, insurance, cars etc.)

_____ $ _____
_____ _____
_____ _____
_____ _____

    Other assets $ _____
    Total assets $ _____

Other liabilities (mortgage, funeral, longer than one year)

_____ $ _____
_____ _____
_____ _____
_____ _____

    Other liabilities $ _____
    Total liabilities $ _____

FAMILY FINANCIAL STATEMENT   Date _____

        Assets   Liabilities

Spouse   Spouse

_____ $ _____   _____ $ _____
_____ _____   _____ _____
_____ _____   _____ _____
_____ _____   _____ _____
_____ _____   _____ _____

    Spouse assets $ _____   Spouse liabilities $ _____

Children   Children

_____ $ _____   _____ $ _____
_____ _____   _____ _____
_____ _____   _____ _____
_____ _____   _____ _____
_____ _____   _____ _____
_____ _____   _____ _____

_____	_____	_____	_____
_____	_____	_____	_____
_____	_____	_____	_____
_____	_____	_____	_____
_____	_____	_____	_____
_____	_____	_____	_____
Family Assets	$ _____	Family liabilities	$ _____
My total assets	+ _____	My total liabilities	+ _____
Family total assets	$ _____	Family total liabilities	$ _____

NET WORTH CALCULATIONS

My net worth: Liquid

    Liquid Assets $ _____

    Current Liab. — _____

    Liquid net worth $ _____

My total net worth

    Total Assets $ _____

    Total Liab. — _____

    Net Worth $ _____

Family net worth

    Family total assets $ _____

    Family total liabilities — _____

    Family Net Worth = $ _____

Miscellaneous information and instructions

_____

_____

_____

_____

_____

_____

_____

_____

_____

_____

_____

_____

_____

_____

EXHIBIT I Worksheet. **EXPENSE APPROXIMATER (Sample).**

Primary	Examples		Now	1st full ret. yr.	Major change years *	**
		Year:				
		Age:				
Housing	Mortgage, rent					
Taxes & Payroll Deductions	Real Estate					
	Federal Income					
	State Income					
	FICA					
	Stock purchase					
	Bond purchase					
Utilities	Telephone					
	Electricity					
	Gas					
	Trash, water, sewer					
Insurance	Vehicles					
	House & Personal Property					
	Life, accident & travel					
Contributions	Church, charity & gifts					
Medical	Net after insurance					
	Health insurance		(company paid)			
Household	Family clothing					
	Food, supplies, etc.					
	House & grounds					
Transportaion	Gas, service & depreciation					
	Commuting (if not with car)					
Personal needs	Cleaning, laundry, etc.					
	Lunch at work					
Recreation	Entertainment					
	Vacations, club dues, etc.					
Education	Tuition, room, board, fees					
Debts	Long & Short Term Paymts					
Miscellaneous	Pets, one-time purchases, other					
Savings	From salary, interest, dividends					
	Total expenses					
	Annual income					
	Long- or short-fall					

* Mortgage paid: extra exemption; life insurance paid.

** Spouse 65: extra exemption.

EXHIBIT III Worksheet. **TAX ESTIMATER (Sample).**

	Year:		
	Age:		

Federal Income Tax

    Salary
    Private Pension (Company Plan)
    Rental Income
    Dividends (Taxable)
    Interest (Taxable)
    Capital Gains (Net Taxable)

       (A) Taxable Income

    Less deductions:
       Rental expenses (Tax, Insurance)
       Itemized Deductions (or 16%)
       Dividend Exclusion
       Dependent Exemptions ($750 × Number)

       (B) Total Deductions

Income Subject to Tax (A−B)

Tax (from Current IRS Tables)

State and County Income Tax (Md.)

    Taxable Income (Federal)
       Additions
       Subtractions
       Itemized Deductions
       Dependent Exemptions ($800 × Number)

    Net Taxable Income

    Tax on First $3000
    Plus 7½% of Remainder

       Total State and County Tax

EXHIBIT V Worksheet. **SOURCES OF "NEW" MONEY (Sample).**

		Year: Age:			
	1. Savings—continue FICA from salary: $100 per pay period for 7 months (9 years)				
(XT)	2. Spouse Earnings and IRA— $1000 per year for 8 years				
	3. Interest on checking account— $2000 × 5% = $100 per year for 8 years				
(XT)	4. Tax savings—shift to tax-free: $300 × 40% tax bracket for 8 years				
	5. Increase return on investment—$7000 × ¾% for 8 years				
	6. Company 25-year service gift— $1000 for 4 years (rec'd in 1980)				
	7. Deferred vacation payment— 65 + days				
	8. Convert insurance program to term and invest balance				
	Total "new" money				